FROM EDEN TO PARADISE

ROSS GREGORY

First published in 2018 by:
Britain's Next Bestseller
An imprint of
Live It Ventures LTD
27 Old Gloucester Road London. WC1N 3AX
Copyright © 2018 by Ross Gregory

The moral right of Ross Gregory to be identified as the author of this work has been asserted by him in accordance with the Copyright, Designs and Patents Act 1988.
All rights reserved.
No part of this book may be reproduced or transmitted in any form or any means without written permission from the copyright holder, except by a reviewer who may quote brief passages in connection with a review for insertion in a newspaper, magazine, website, or broadcast.
A catalogue record for this book is available from the British Library.
All characters appearing in this work are fictitious. Any resemblance to real persons, living or dead, is purely coincidental.
www.bnbsbooks.co.uk
@BNBSbooks
Cover design: Ross Gregory
ISBN 978-1-910565-66-7
Printed in the U.K
Photographs by Peter Talbot

To Nikola, Cole and Cerys for all that you've done in helping me complete my first (and possibly only!) book, fulfilling a lifelong ambition. Without your understanding, love and support this project would have remained just a dream.

FOREWORD

BY JULIO ARCA

I must admit, I didn't know much about South Shields Football Club when I signed for them in 2015.

I'd been playing a bit of Sunday League football after I retired but was then approached by Jon King asking if I could come and have a look at the club, talk to them and see what I thought.

We talked for about five or six weeks, negotiating, myself and the club. It was a starting point for them - something new for them. They'd been getting players in from the Northern League but were looking to get some different players in as well, and there was the idea with me to attract more people to the club.

You could see the first game I played, against Stokesley, that the crowd had grown, then slowly we started growing the fanbase. I don't think anyone would have predicted how quickly it would take off, though.

It took me a few months to realise the potential. I knew South Shields was a big place with a lot of Sunderland and Newcastle fans but I didn't know how much interest there would be from fans to come and watch football in that division. It was a gamble in a way by Geoff Thompson, the chairman, but these people can see when something has potential. Now look at the club. It has probably grown quicker than he thought, in every aspect, on the pitch and outside.

FOREWORD

I come from a normal town with working-class people. Football didn't change me in that way and I still respect people. The time these people put into the club, for free, you have to respect that. They didn't get paid and the hours, wow, some of them were there every day trying to get the pitch right, get the club right. People see the players out there, playing hard, and they think 'great, we won today' but they don't see what's happening behind us.

It happens everywhere, those people behind the scenes. The higher you go, they don't work for free but if you go to Sunderland Football Club, there's a groundsman who does a hell of a lot of work there and they are under pressure, but the fans don't always see that support the players get.

That's why personally, I respect all of these people because while the chairman may be putting the money in without all of these people it would be hard to maintain the club.

It's been an incredible rise for South Shields FC. It has been crazy. The club went in 24 months from playing at Peterlee in front of a dozen people to playing at Wembley with 18,000 fans there.

That's how quick the club has grown and it shows they has done the right things. They have invested in the right players, invested in the right areas off the pitch, they've got an academy going on and there is so much going on. It's getting bigger and bigger.

Playing for South Shields was a whole different experience to what I'd had in the Premier League, Championship, Sunday League, a whole different chapter in my life that went better than I ever thought. The last few years has gone better than anyone probably ever thought.

You don't see many ex-pros playing in the Northern League but I committed 100 per cent to the club, on the pitch and off it. I've loved being at this club, helping promote it. I can't speak highly enough of it.

I didn't know about the FA Vase until a couple of months after I'd been there. I didn't know much about the Northern League to be fair. It was more that I just wanted to play and keep myself fit. We were only training once or twice a week so it wasn't taking up much of my time.

But then the more time I spent there, the more I learned about the club, found out what the club had been through. There were so many people who had been there for many, many years and you start to appreciate what they've been through.

It's not like it changed your performance but when you went out to play for South Shields, you realise you don't just want to do it for yourself, you want to do it for them too. They were there when the club didn't have anything at all.

It started getting better and better for myself, the feeling that you are representing all of these people.

They deserve the success South Shields has had over the last few years more than anyone else.

PROLOGUE

SATURDAY, MARCH 1 2013 SOUTH SHIELDS 0-0 WILLINGTON

THIS WASN'T HOW GOD IMAGINED EDEN, SURELY.

It's far from paradise for South Shields Football Club, that much is sure.

Gary Crutwell examines the raffle takings, emptying the few coins onto the table in the committee room, pushing and prodding them around. Not much there, but then when you've had a crowd of 45 people, what can you expect?

It's been seven, long months since South Shields FC were turfed out of the town. Homeless, almost penniless.

Another dark stain on a tumultuous history.

South Shields Football Club in name, now, but little else. Now playing 25 miles away at Peterlee's Eden Lane. Surviving but little more.

Crutwell pushes the coins around again, counting them a second time, then a third, in the hope that he may have miscalculated. Outside, the referee and two linesmen - assistants, whatever you want to call them these days - are waiting to be paid.

They'd had little to do that bitter, windswept Saturday. It had been South Shields' first game for more than two months after a particularly cruel winter had decimated their fixture list and the players were understandably ring-rusty.

Long-serving striker Stephen Ramsey had thudded a header off the crossbar, Adam Burnicle twice denied by Moffatt in the Willington goal.

At the other end, veteran Simon Parkin was making his first appearance in South Shields colours since December 2011 as injuries and availability hit hard the threadbare squad. Manager Jon King had called on the 38-year-old as a favour and was rewarded with a clean sheet.

It was about the only bonus that could be taken from a game that had done little to persuade spectators that the 50-mile round trip was worth making.

TUESDAY, APRIL 26 2016 SOUTH SHIELDS 5-0 WILLINGTON

Julio Arca, more than 300 Premier League appearances under his belt, grabs the large, silver trophy, lifts it aloft high above his head and roars. All around him, the cheers are echoed by the 1,000-strong crowd who have stayed to watch him.

It was a late finish. A floodlight failure at Mariners Park had threatened to spoil the title party but the generator had finally kicked back into life after 45 minutes in the dark.

This time.

Willington, again the opposition. This time no need for coin-counting, barrel-scraping, teeth-gnashing.

South Shields were back. Back home, back in the town, back on track.

SUNDAY, MAY 21 2017 SOUTH SHIELDS 4-0 CLEETHORPES TOWN

King Street has long had a desolate, deserted feeling. Footfall has been dwindling on South Shields' main shopping street for the last decade.

Big retailers have shut up and moved on. Marks & Spencer, Internacionale, Mothercare. Even Greggs shut their cafe, though they still have a couple of outlets providing sarnies, steak bakes and sausage rolls to the hardcore still shopping there.

But there are even fewer people treading King Street today. Fewer too on the promenade and beach, despite the sunny weather which normally brings folk flocking to the dunes.

Three-hundred-and-fifty miles away, Wembley Stadium. Twenty-thousand Sand Dancers jumping, singing. The South Shields boys making all the noise, everywhere they go.

May 21, 2017. Shields is a ghost town. Yet still, if you listen closely enough, you can still hear a buzz.

CHAPTER ONE

M‍AY 21, 2017... THE SUN SHONE ON WEMBLEY, AS IT ALWAYS seems to do.

Unless you're Steve McClaren, perhaps.

There was no need for a brolly on this Sunday lunchtime, nor were there any wallies on show. Certainly not in maroon and blue.

And boy, there was plenty maroon and blue. From the press box view, across the other side of the great stadium, a sea of South Shields colours swamped the stand, dancing, singing, chanting and cheering.

Conservative estimates had the number at 15,000.

To their right, the Cleethorpes Town fans were doing their best to match the noise but with less than 2,000 among their number, it was a pointless, thankless task.

"Everywhere we go, everywhere we go… the South Shields boys, making all the noise, everywhere we go."

The song rang out in force, as it had less than 24 hours earlier at Covent Garden when the invasion had been in full force. A balmy, summer-like afternoon had needed no second invitation for the Mariners fans as they descended in force on London town.

The capital has seen many a sight from football fans. The experience is not new for the bars, pubs, staff and police but this was an entirely new experience for South Shields fans. Most had never travelled to London for a game. They knew for a club of their size to reach the final was something that may never happen again, certainly not for a long time.

They were here to enjoy it, party and make it not just an unforgettable day but a memorable weekend.

How many of them can remember that Saturday afternoon and evening, though, will be open to debate. I'd had the pleasure of travelling down to London that day with the team, with a mid-afternoon stop-off at Aston Villa's training ground breaking up the journey before we finally arrived at the hotel in Ealing around 5pm. A quick shower and change of clothes, a couple of pints in the bar, and before long we were on the way to Covent Garden in a taxi with some of the club's committee who were equally desperate to witness the scenes that were unfolding.

Social media was going mental with pictures of thousands of Mariners lining the streets, spilling out of bars, full of drink and song and when we finally landed the party was in full swing.

Proud Sand Dancer Phil Brown, the Southend United manager, was tucking into a pint surrounded by well-wishers. He wasn't hard to miss even among the crowd, with the former Hull City boss and Sam Allardyce's sidekick at Bolton dressed in a Hawaiian shirt and bright orange trousers that almost matched his skin colour.

Very dashing, Phil, but even you can't take the spotlight away from the Shields fans. Not tonight.

Round the corner, the bedlam hit you like a Julio Arca free-kick.

Mason's Bar, on Henrietta Street, was the place to be. Ran by a Shields woman, it had been earmarked as the meeting place for fans and the place had responded in style, with maroon and blue balloons, drinks offers and more.

It was large inside but nowhere near big enough to house the hordes who had descended upon it. Instead, the street outside was lined with punters, waving scarves and full of spirit. And beer. And cider.

Someone, from somewhere, had got their hands on a football and every few seconds it was punted up in the air, then headed, kicked, punched across the crowd to 'ole, ole'. Cars struggling to get down the street had to inch forward while the crowd parted to let them past. The sound of tooting horns wasn't in annoyance, but in celebration as the drivers gave thumbs up and shook hands through their windows with the fans on the street.

It was all fun and frolics, with little hint of trouble despite Sunderland and Newcastle United supporters mixing together. Only later on in the night, when a few songs went up inside Masons, could a slight edge be felt in the atmosphere. One baby-faced youngster, who didn't look old enough to be watching CBeebies on his own never mind drinking in a Covent Garden pub, seemed intent on aggravation but he was soon shouted down by the rest of the bar.

But that was what the beauty of the weekend was. No tribal rivalries, no bother or trouble. No hooliganism.

Contrast the behaviour of 15,000 Sand Dancers with what went on earlier that same Saturday when the League One play-off final had ended with Millwall fans invading the Wembley turf at the final whistle after they had beaten Bradford City. Hundreds of supporters spilled onto the pitch, running up to the Bradford players and goading, threatening them in a horrible incident which even left Lions match-winner Steve Morison sickened just five minutes after his goal had left him feeling on top of the world.

"I have never been so high and so low in such a short period of time," he told reporters afterwards. "I don't want the headlines to be about them, it should be about us.

"And those people who have ruined it for everyone else should hang their heads in shame."

Unfortunately for Morison and his team-mates, that play-off game will now only be remembered for a mindless group of supporters.

Once again, Millwall had destroyed a Wembley experience for their club. It's not as if they haven't got previous, however. Twelve months earlier they'd been at Wembley again, this time losing 3-1 to Barnsley in the 2016 League One play-off final. Their response? Trying to charge through a line of stewards and into the Barnsley section of fans to attack them when the third goal went in.

But that's Millwall. Often talked about as a 'minority spoiling it for everyone else', their reputation now precedes them.

Shields are coming from a lower level, where the Northern League, in the main, is seen as a place for camaraderie and enjoyment, not hooliganism. That's not to say some clubs don't have an element, but they are so few and far between to not deserve a mention. Instead, despite the rivalry that clearly exists, there is still support and a desire to see other Northern League clubs do well in national competitions. While Shields may have had a fair amount of jealousy and bitterness directed at them, there remained a sense of loyalty to a fellow club from the area.

Within that huge crowd for the FA Vase Final, there were fans and committee men, managers and players from other clubs. Some may have turned up just for the day out; indeed one rival manager told me he'd come to cheer on Cleethorpes. But in the main, they were there to support the Mariners, just as the hardcore Shields fans were, the 'glory-hunters', and the Newcastle and Sunderland fans who were desperate to see a North East team they could support achieve Wembley glory for once!

Despite all these different factions, despite all these varying reasons for turning up and strained loyalties, there wasn't a pick of bother. While the players did themselves proud out on the pitch, off it the Shields following more than matched them - and made it a standout weekend.

Graham Fenton and Lee Picton had a couple of big calls to make prior to kick-off, and in the professional manner in which they approached almost every aspect of every game during the season, they decided to make them on Saturday, rather than delay it until the morning of the game.

The build-up to the Vase final had been long. A month had gone by since the Coleshill victory had booked the club's first-ever visit to Wembley but a lot of football had been played since, including three cup finals. The management duo were adamant that once the semi-final had gone, there was a blank sheet of paper which needed each and every player to force their name to be written on it for May 21.

Well, almost every player. Liam Connell was nailed on to play given - bar coach Simon Parkin - he was the only goalkeeper eligible. But elsewhere, places were up for grabs.

The team that started the second leg against Coleshill was:

Connell; Baxter, Morse, Shaw, Lough; Briggs, Arca, Phillips, Stephenson; Foley, Cogdon. How many of that XI would keep their places for Wembley? At the time, that seemed Fenton and Picton's first-choice side, even when everyone was fit. Yes, Carl Finnigan's form could warrant a spot. Michael Richardson, who missed the Coleshill game with tonsillitis, would be challenging Andrew Stephenson for the No 10 role and there were a number of players on the fringes of the starting team that could push for an opportunity in the coming games but if the Wembley team had to be picked there and then, it would have been a knocking bet the second-leg side would have been selected again.

A week is a long time in football, however, never mind a month. Injuries can strike, form can dip or rise. That was the challenge laid down by the management duo: play your way into the team.

And as the games went by, suddenly the starting XI looked less clear-cut. Morse had limped off in the last few seconds of the league win at North Shields and wasn't seen again; likewise Baxter faced a race to be fit in time after breaking his hand a couple of weeks earlier.

The unluckiest break of all, though, was Stephen Ramsey's leg fracture at Sunderland RCA. The long-serving striker was celebrating his tenth season at the club, having stuck by them through thick and thin. While he wouldn't have started at Wembley, his dreams of a place on the bench and a potential substitute appearance had died.

Finnigan had shoved his name forward for a start with his performances in the run-in, particularly the League Cup Final against North Shields. Stephenson, too, had been the stand-out player in the Durham Challenge Cup Final but could both play behind a front two of Cogdon and Foley, whose form meant they were certainties to start? Or would one be utilised on the right of the midfield diamond, putting Rob Briggs' place in jeopardy?

So many dilemmas but for Picton and Fenton, their minds were clear. Rather than waiting until the morning of the game to inform the players, they told them on Saturday night at the hotel, pulling them in one by one.

We were still out in Covent Garden but a text came through to

Gazette reporter Liam Kennedy from Finnigan, a good pal of his from their days playing and covering Dundee. It simply said 'I'm starting'.

One piece of the jigsaw in place. If Finnigan was starting, it had to be in the No 10 role which meant Richardson missing out. The guess went up that Stephenson would get the nod on the right ahead of Briggs, whose form hadn't been as strong the last few weeks. It turned out to be the right guess.

It was harsh on Briggs, who had a bad experience on his only other visit to Wembley when he was part of the West Auckland side that lost the Vase final to Sholing in 2014. His goal in the quarter-final at Mariners Park, a thunderbolt that finished off a sweeping team move, was one of the highlights of the Vase run.

"It was the hardest and lowest point of the weekend, and potentially the season," admitted Picton. "We've got a group of players who have been outstanding pretty much across the board all season long, and to have to tell some of those players that their hopes and dreams of starting at Wembley are shattered in this particular instance was a real tough moment for us.

"But what I will say is that it was a measure of the quality of personality that we've got within our dressing room is that the lads took that disappointment. Some of them came on the pitch, some of them didn't, but they all played their part. There was nobody sulking in the background, we came together as a group and I'm immensely proud of that.

"I don't think you could have picked an XI where people would have said there's no surprises there. Because we've got such strength in depth in our squad, no matter which XI we picked there would always be a percentage of the fanbase who would go 'I was expecting him to play'.

"You could argue that there were a couple of lads on the bench who if you looked at things over the course of a season might have potentially deserved to start but we said we weren't going to pick a team based on how they played three months ago, we were going to pick a team based on the closest games to the final itself."

I'd spoken at length with Fenton in the build-up about his times at Wembley both as a player and manager. He had experience of dropping players from the starting XI for North Shields, and also being 17th man at Wembley for the League Cup Final in 2000 when at Leicester City, a fate that ultimately fell on Romanian Iulian Petrache for the Mariners.

"It's not nice being part of that process, but you have to make that decision as a coach or manager," said Fenton.

"Some people really stuck their necks out and it was more to do with people doing well rather than people not doing well. The people we left out had still been playing well, still contributing hugely but unfortunately you can only pick eleven people and that was the midfield four we went with."

Briggs was devastated. As an employee of BT, he was supposed to do a special interview with BT Sport - who were broadcasting the final live - before the game but ducked out of it. He was to put his heartache to one side, however, with a superb cameo from the bench in the second half.

Equally as upset was Petrache. The centre-half was always going to miss out on the squad but if everyone else seemed to know it, he didn't and his father had flown over from Romania to see his son in action.

Baxter ultimately didn't recover from his broken wrist in time, but Morse proved his fitness. Alex Nicholson came in at right-back while the rest of the side picked itself, leading to a starting XI of: Connell; Nicholson, Morse, Shaw, Lough; Stephenson, Arca, Phillips, Finnigan; Cogdon, Foley. Subs: Richardson, Briggs, Smith, Storey, Holden.

It was always likely to be strong enough... and so it proved.

———

CLEETHORPES WERE huge underdogs going into the final. Shields had them watched and - to be blunt - weren't impressed.

Nor was the Northern League's press officer Mike Snowdon who had travelled down to Grimsby one midweek evening to watch the Northern Counties East League side in action and returned to say: "If Shields don't win by at least four then there's something wrong."

Mike would have been just as well served putting the lottery numbers on that weekend too, as his words became prophetic.

What Shields wanted was an early goal, but it didn't arrive. For the spectacle of the game it was probably for the best as if it had, the floodgates could have opened and the result may have been out of sight before half-time.

Finnigan was thriving in his role just off the frontmen, and had two early opportunities to open the scoring, failing to scramble home Stephenson's header down inside the six yard box before being denied by Cleethorpes goalkeeper Liam Higton after a Cogdon through ball.

He wasn't to be denied, however, when Cogdon was clipped in the box and a penalty was awarded. Three minutes before half-time, Finnigan slipped the ball to the keeper's right to have the honour of being the first South Shields player to score at Wembley.

Not the first player from South Shields, of course. The most famous Sand Dancer of all, Stan Mortensen, still holds the record of being the only man to score a hat-trick in an FA Cup Final, his incredible feat coming more than 60 years ago in 1953.

Finnigan could have replicated that inside the first half, while after the break another South Shields-born player, David Foley, was just inches away from his own hat-trick. Foley had already hammered a long-range effort against the crossbar before he grabbed goals number three and four late in the second half to put the gloss on the win.

The man for the big occasion again, Foley ran through in the 86th minute to slot home after a killer pass from Richardson and two minutes later, rifled home his 35th goal of the season. Incredibly, after such a season, it was his last real contribution to the club. A few weeks later he'd be gone, off to Spennymoor in acrimonious circumstances after the club announced he'd moved for more money.

His contribution to the season was immense and his link-up with Gavin Cogdon in attack dispelled any notion that two small guys can't play up front together. The duo, both diminutive in stature, terrified defences all season long to show that size doesn't matter when you have such ability in your feet and a football brain to go with it.

Cogdon was sensational at Wembley. A scorer on his last visit there for Spennymoor in 2013, he somehow didn't get on the scoresheet this time, rattling the post just before the interval and generally torturing the right side of the Cleethorpes defence when he peeled out wide. If anyone deserved the man of the match trophy it was him, but the official honour fell to Wayne Phillips. He was nominated by Morpeth boss Nicky Gray, who was co-commentating for BT Sport while sporting a white suit jacket which appeared to be some sort of homage to the Liverpool 1996 FA Cup Final team. Within a fortnight of that award, Phillips had signed for Gray.

Perhaps the goal of the game, in many ways, was the second. With the Mariners ahead by just a slender margin, they encountered a few jitters, no more so than when Cleethorpes' main danger-man Brody Robertson broke clean through and looked set to equalise, only for Nicholson to produce a superb last-ditch block as he was about to pull the trigger. As good as a goal, that moment shouldn't be underestimated.

The second goal, when it arrived, looked so simple but was the epitome of what Lee Picton, Graham Fenton and Martin Scott had been doing behind the scenes. Set-piece isn't a dirty word but for many football followers, working on them in training is almost seen as crude coaching. The likes of Tony Pulis, Sam Allardyce and George Graham became associated with negativity through their perceived reliance on set-pieces, but like it or not, free-kicks and corners are a huge part of football and a golden opportunity to score a goal.

Fenton, in particular, takes a particular interest in them. Videos of opposition set-ups at set-pieces are often used in Shields training sessions, and the work on delivery, the runs made, positioning and blocking is drummed into players.

No more so than the last session before the final.

Stopping off at Bodymoor Heath, the state-of-the art training ground owned by Fenton's old club Aston Villa, the players were put through a warm-up by Scott before Fenton took over. Instructing the players on a couple of corner kick routines, he then moved on to a free-kick drill he wanted them to work on. It involved a couple of players making nuisances of themselves in the wall before offering an option for a slide pass down the side, while centre-halves Shaw and Morse peeled off toward the back post, with Morse blocking the defenders to allow Shaw a free run.

The chance to put it into practice arrived in the 68th minute. Briggs stood over the ball, Cogdon and Foley were busy around the wall while the two Shields defenders and Richardson looked for the cross.

It worked like a dream. Well, almost. The defence was distracted, Shaw peeled round to the far post but just as he looked set to head home from close range, Morse appeared in front of him to grab the glory, nodding in the killer goal from a matter of yards out.

Practice makes perfect.

Just about.

Shaw had spoken in the build-up about his dream as a boy of scoring at Wembley, but the striker-turned-defender couldn't complain at being pipped by his young defensive partner.

"The set-piece we worked on, it is me who scores the header," laughed Shaw afterwards. "Dillon made the perfect movement to step away and then, as I make the longer run, block my defender. But instead of doing that he decided to come and get a goal instead! I'm shouting for it, I'm about to head it and then he just gets there. But listen, I love that kid, he is like my son, and I'm not going to begrudge him that goal at Wembley. Yes, I'm gutted not to score, but I'll take that clean sheet!"

So 4-0... and as comfortable a victory as you're likely to see. Cleethorpes were game opponents but ultimately well short of the quality needed to stop the juggernaut in its tracks.

Four goals, four trophies. "Four-midable", as the Gazette headline read.

The end of a fantastic story in some ways; yet in others, it has only just begun.

CHAPTER TWO

November 4, 2013...

The fog crept in over the North Sea, drifting silently like a ghostly apparition.

Two miles inset, the death of a once-famous club looked inevitable as the mist enveloped Eden Lane, settling over a damp, miserable Northern League Two game.

The hardy souls who had braved the elements pulled their collars up, fastened down hoods and hats. Inside a small hut, Bob Wray moved the portable gas heater closer to him, warmed his gloved hands by it, a sickening feeling in the pit of his stomach. He pulled away from the warmth, peering out of the door to see if anyone else was on their way down to his makeshift turnstile.

There wasn't.

He counted the takings, not that it took long. Twelve paying punters had passed through his gate. Not enough to pay the match officials, barely enough to cover the cost of the post-match grub. The official attendance would later say 67 but with a mixture of free passes and committee men it painted a distorted picture.

Bob was approaching 80. Club historian, supporters' club secretary and chief fundraiser, he had seen it all before at South Shields. From the Simonside Hall heyday post-war to the club going extinct when it was swallowed up and spat out by Gateshead. Twice. The reformation, gates locked when teams had turned up for games at Filtrona Park, cup winning days and now this.

"The real bad time was that Tuesday night against Esh Winning when I was on the gate," Bob recalled. "There was fog, there was rain and I was in the gatehouse. Gary Crutwell got me a gas fire and I had a little light in there and all I had to do was flog the tickets and programmes.

"I had to sell raffle tickets, programmes and take the entrance money all at the same time. That tells you there wasn't much of a rush in those days.

"We had 12 paying punters against Esh and that was the low point. It was soul-destroying. I was nearly in tears. How had it come to this?"

Just exactly how it had come to this was a long, torturous process, another exasperatingly-convoluted affair in the rollercoaster life of South Shields FC. This particular chapter in the history of the Mariners started in 1992 with the purchase of Filtrona Park by John Rundle, a local businessman and chairman of the football club.

Shields had been playing at the council-owned Jack Clark Park for 18 years, operating in the Wearside League after the blow of losing their famous Simonside Hall home. Various potential sites had been looked at as a new home, in a situation which was to have startling echoes with what was to come, but it wasn't until 1992 that the sports club and ground of Filtrona FC became available. Standing redundant and vandalised, it had previously been the home of the works team of the next-door factory which specialised in filter products for the cigarette industry.

For Rundle, it was both a business opportunity and the chance to relocate the football club. Along with some family members, he stumped up the asking price and bought the five-acre plot, which had a pitch, a clubhouse and vast land for potential development.

Over the years, Filtrona Park was gradually upgraded and redeveloped to turn it into one of the most promising grounds in the region and on the pitch, South Shields moved out of the Wearside League and gained promotion to the historic Northern League.

A new home, a new era, but the same old issues seemed to dog the football club.

Twice, South Shields had ceased to be, merging with Gateshead, in 1930 and 1974, who had taken their place - and name. The club had risen from the ashes on those occasions, building itself back up but by 2006, the future was in real doubt again. By this time, Rundle had grown weary of running the team. Fall-outs with the committee and side followed, as did his resignation as chairman but as owner of the ground, he still had a considerable hand to play. On Saturday, February 4, 2006, South Shields were set to face Alnwick Town in a Division Two clash. Both sets of players and management turned up at Filtrona Park, only to find the gates locked. Access was refused and the game didn't go ahead.

Once again, the very existence was threatened.

A new committee was formed and a new chairman, Gary Crutwell, was found from the thriving Sunday football scene in the town. The team picked up on the pitch, new manager Gary Steadman filled his matchday squad with local talent and promotion was finally secured in 2008 and, two years later, the League Cup lifted thanks to a pulsating penalty shoot-out victory over Ashington at Dunston, Richard Paxton slotting home the winning spot-kick to hand the Mariners their first silverware in 15 years.

Off the field, though, it was still a struggle, with the ever-present threat of Rundle selling Filtrona Park. For chairman Gary Crutwell & Co, the need to either raise enough capital to buy the ground, or find a new home, was always at the forefront of their minds.

The summer of 2011 was the start of a long, painful exit from the club. Now aged 73, Rundle wanted to retire, sell up and move on. Filtrona Park was put up for sale, initially at a price of £399,999 and the club was told it would either have to buy or move on. At the end of the 2011-12 campaign the team, now under the management of Jon King, finished 13th in Northern League Division One, but there was no movement off the pitch.

Crutwell and the committee had worked tirelessly behind the scenes, having meetings with banks and mortgage companies. The price had come down to £310,000 but by the summer of 2012 they were short of the deposit needed to secure a mortgage by around £40,000. Talks with the local council, including leader Iain Malcolm, were under way to try and find another venue. The historic Gypsies Green had long been touted as a possible alternative, but would need considerable resource to upgrade the facility, home of South Shields Harriers and a meeting place for finishers at the end of the Great North Run.

Shields were now technically homeless. Even if they could secure Gypsies Green, the vast amount of work needed to get it up to Northern League standard meant they would need to groundshare for a season with another club.

David Miliband, former Foreign Secretary and once golden boy of New Labour, at the time was MP for the town and vice-president of the football club. He jumped into the fight, negotiating with the council and local businesses to try and safeguard the future of the club but even the persuasive powers of a man once tipped as Tony Blair's successor at 10 Downing Street seemed to be in vain.

With just days to go until the new season started, the club reached a new agreement with Rundle to continue playing at Filtrona for one more season. The owner had been unsuccessful in his attempts to flog the ground, with initial interest from a couple of parties, including rugby league outfit Gateshead Thunder, coming to nothing. Rundle would have been left with a huge white elephant. The football club, meanwhile, had seen their last hope of a groundshare fall through at the beginning of the week. Both parties' hands were forced and back round the negotiating table, a deal was struck.

"We were looking at going out of business," said Crutwell. "It really was Filtrona or bust."

It gave the club the breathing space to try and realise the funds needed to acquire the ground again, with Rundle emphasising this was for one more season, and one season alone.

He was good to his word.

Over the next few months, more efforts were made to raise enough capital to realise a mortgage for Filtrona. Bob Wray and the Supporters' Club set up a share scheme with Ward Hadaway Solicitors, appealing to the community to buy into the project and retain a club in South Shields, but apathy reigned. Take up was poor and the proposal, launched in a blaze of publicity in the Shields Gazette and local media, went down with a whimper.

So it seemed would the football club.

Given a year's grace, efforts were stepped up but two major blows left the club on its knees. In October 2012, committee man Kevin Law, a major financial contributor and one of the key players alongside Crutwell, died suddenly aged just 50. It was a hammer blow, doubled with the news that Miliband, having lost the race to be Labour leader to his little brother a couple of years previous, had decided to quit politics, and South Shields, to move to New York where he would head up the International Rescue Committee. The irony was not lost on many who had seen his efforts to rescue the Mariners fail to bear fruition.

Minus one of the driving forces of their campaign, and their biggest political ally, it was no wonder the bid ran out of steam. On the field, the uncertainty took its toll too and Shields finished second bottom, relegated on a bitterly cold night at Consett (is there any other types of night in Consett?). They finished the season with 38 points, having used 65 players.

The final game of the campaign, and the last at Filtrona Park as it stood, was a derby against Hebburn Town. Their neighbours, traditionally in the shadow of the 'bigger club', finished 15 points better off than Shields in their first season back in Division One, culminating in a 2-0 win in the last game of the season. The attendance was just 106. Shields had averaged 163 that tumultuous term. The next time the two teams were to meet on Shaftesbury Avenue, the crowd was 1,827.

Scott Robson and Stuart Nicholson, a player with brief Premier League experience at West Bromwich Albion, were on target. They were to be the last Northern League goals scored at the ground for 28 months.

Shields were homeless again, and this time there would be no last-gasp negotiations. John Rundle, true to his word, had given them 12 months to come up with the finances to buy Filtrona Park but it wasn't happening.

At the end of the season, Shields had to plan not only for life in Division Two, but also possibly for life outside of the Northern League, perhaps dropping into the Wearside League, or even going out of existence if a ground couldn't be found.

CHAPTER THREE

June 18, 2013...

Vice-chairman Phil Thornton issues a statement confirming South Shields FC WILL have a team next season... playing 'home' games some 20 miles away in Peterlee.

A temporary reprieve. Not ideal, but beggars can't be choosers.

You could almost hear the relief in his voice as Thornton said: "We are delighted that we have been able to secure the use of Eden Lane in Peterlee for the coming season, and would like to take this opportunity to thank Peterlee Council for its fantastic support throughout this process.

"With the groundshare in place and our Northern League status secured, we can now begin to focus fully on our long-term plans regarding a new home for the club, back in South Shields, for the 2014/15 season."

It would take a bit longer than that but what the club's committee had done was secure the short-term future of the historic club and bought some time.

Having held their collective breath for so long, they could finally suck in large gasps of air, filling their lungs knowing that they would live to fight another day.

The summer of 2013 had been one of the most difficult, most

fraught in the club's history.

Homeless and in real danger of going out of existence, the club's loyal band of committee men explored every avenue possible to ensure there would still be a Northern League team with the name South Shields.

Negotiations continued with the council over possible temporary homes at Gypsies Green or a return to Jack Clark Park, but neither were up to Northern League standard. If they were to remain at that level, a groundshare would have to be found.

Several options were considered, and then ruled out. Harton and Westoe's ground, which could have seen them stay in the town, wasn't up to Northern League standard. Hebburn Town's Sports and Social Club ground was a no-go because of the cricket and other games played there. A chance to play at Washington's Albany Park fell through and things looked bleak, until one remaining option appeared left on the table, down the road at Boldon CA's Villa Ground.

Boldon CA were competing in the Wearside League but had ambitions to become a Northern League side, installing floodlights and developing their ground so that should success emerge on the pitch, they would be in a position to take promotion. The ground wasn't quite up to standard but not far off, and the South Shields committee were sure that with a bit of elbow grease and hard work, they could get it ready for the start of the season.

Long-serving committee man David Fall, secretary Phil Reay and Gary Crutwell were all involved in the deal - and it seemed to be a real possibility. Suddenly, things were looking up, providing the proposal could be ratified.

The CA committee included several representatives, including Jarrow Roofing FC owner Richie McLoughlin. A businessman and football fanatic, McLoughlin has ploughed hundreds of thousands of pounds of his money into creating his own football club, running it as chairman, manager, secretary and groundsman, and Roofing's Boldon Sports Ground sat 50 yards opposite the Villa.

The committee met, discussed the proposal and rejected it.

"Boldon CA were on the bones of their backside at the same time," said Fall. "Phil and I attended the meeting with their people, we organised the deal, we were going to do a little bit to their stand, put a toilet in for them, all this to bring it up to standard.

"That was all agreed but it had to go to the Boldon CA executive, and I'll not mince my words, them buggers boycotted it and threw it out so we were back to bloody square one."

It was an incident which soured relations between football folk in the borough, some of which have never fully recovered. Shields felt abandoned and let down by the football community in South Tyneside.

There was just one hope left, but instead of moving somewhere else in South Shields, or even the borough, it was 25 miles down the A19 at Peterlee. Eden Lane had been the home of Peterlee Town in the Northern League until 2011. The club, changing its name to Peterlee Newtown, had limped along in the Wearside League for another couple of seasons but at the end of the 2012-13 campaign, had folded.

A vacant ground, not far off the required standard but far, far away from South Tyneside. It wasn't ideal, but needs must when the devil's pissing on your chips.

It was team manager Jon King who first heard of Peterlee possibly being a saviour. Still playing on a Sunday morning, a chance conversation in the changing rooms put Shields on their way to Eden Lane.

"How that came along was I was playing on a Sunday morning for Glen Liddle at the Biddick Inn," said King. "Glen had come in as my assistant at Shields when Davie Hagan left and I'd been helping out playing in the Gateshead & District League.

"When we found out at the end of the season that we wouldn't have a ground, nobody could help us. Washington, who we'd given nets to previously when they'd had a fire, they wouldn't help us. We got sorted out to go to Boldon then someone put the spanner in at the last minute and that got stopped. The only team that was probably going to let us play was Durham City, but it was going to cost us something crazy like £500 a week to go there, which we couldn't afford.

"I was in the changing room at Biddick one Sunday and the lads were asking what was happening. Another lad, who was assisting

Glen on a Sunday, said he knew a groundsman at Peterlee and their ground was free as they didn't have a team.

"My first thoughts were 'Peterlee, that's miles away' but I told the lad we didn't have anywhere and we'd look at it. I told Gary Crutwell about it and he was hoping to get somewhere closer but he went down and had a chat and the rest is history.

"If I hadn't have been in that changing room that Sunday, we wouldn't have had a club. I'm convinced of that. Nobody would give us anything, the ground wasn't going to happen. It was a stroke of luck as I wasn't at all the games, I was 38 and wasn't playing all the time, the young lads were playing and I didn't go every week.

"If I hadn't have been there, had that conversation, we wouldn't have a team now. South Shields certainly wouldn't have what it's got now."

As 'strokes of luck' go, it's right up there with the best of them. The old saying goes, however, that you make your own luck and golfer Gary Player's maxim that 'the harder I practice, the luckier I get' certainly rings true.

Shields had knocked on so many doors, yet had so many slammed shut in their face, that they deserved a break, no matter how it came.

"We approached Peterlee Council and the rest is history," said Fall. "We had to pay around £900 a year for the pitch and they looked after it.

"We got tremendous support down there, we had meetings with the council who wanted it to be used as it would just lie dormant. The superintendent down there couldn't do enough for us. He organised the deal, the ground itself was in good nick but the stand was condemned but we got that sorted. There was a lot of work from the lads, wire-brushing the steelwork to get rid of rust and coat of paint, but we got that up and running."

The 'lads'.

A group of middle-aged and retired men, some in their seventies, working their fingers to the bone, heavy manual labour, just to keep the club they love alive. A true labour of love.

The Peterlee Posse. Gary Crutwell, David Fall, Phil Reay, Bob Wray, Richard Bailey and Bob Scott. Remember the names because without them, and others such as long-serving vice-president Gerry Reilly, strong committee men like Phil Thornton and Darren Wright, plus the junior member of the team, media man Daniel Prince, there wouldn't be a Wembley trip. Hell, there might not be a club today.

Combined together, they dedicated hundreds of unpaid hours to the cause. For some, it was a labour of love stretching back decades. Bailey had begun supporting the Mariners as a 10-year-old in 1945 after his father Bill returned from the war and seventy years later was still going strong, serving on the committee, sweeping out the changing rooms and tending to the ground on matchdays.

Wray, also, had first watched the club in the late 1940s at their Horsley Hill ground, a majestic old place which housed the football club from 1919 and is the venue for their record crowd, an attendance of 24,348 for the FA Cup fifth round match against Swansea Town on Februray 19, 1927.

Phil Reay, long-time secretary, was easy to spot at Shields games. Just look for the only man in short sleeves and no jacket in the middle of winter. For 15 years, he has been an ever-present figure at first-team fixtures, missing just one game in that time, due to being stuck in hospital. "I wasn't happy. It was a nil-nil draw with Willington. It sounded like a cracker."

Staunch volunteers like the Peterlee Posse are the bedrock of any Northern League football club and without these 'lads' sticking by the club, working their fingers to the bone and risking life and limb at times, the club wouldn't have survived.

"I remember being up a ladder at Peterlee one morning, suffering vertigo at 60," reminisces Bob Scott. "I was convinced I was going to drop this paint everywhere and come crashing down. We ended up getting some staging to get it done."

Bob Wray's not one to be outdone: "What about me, at 75, up a long ladder with a wire brush trying to brush off steel, filling eight bin bags by hand so we could get another year out of the stand which was virtually condemned."

Health and safety clearly wasn't a big concern.

"It was hard work, but we enjoyed it," added Scott. "Hands and knees on the pitch with a bread knife, sticking pieces of turf down. We went home and felt we'd achieved something."

Up and running, but Peterlee was a struggle. Eden Lane was a haven but no bountiful respite.

When times are hard, ingenuity is needed. With no clubhouse of their own to sell beer and raise money, 'the lads' had to think on their feet.

A large, American style fridge, acquired second hand from a neighbour of Wray's who was refurbishing his kitchen, was to be a lifesaver. Shipped 25 miles down the road, it took pride of place in a makeshift bar.

Fall said: "We managed to get one room next door where we would sell cans of beer that we'd bought from the local shop at the bottom of Peterlee and sold for £2.50 a can out of this fridge. That's where we had to get funds from."

All the ideas, ingenuity, cajoling and hard work can't always get people through the gate, though. This was South Shields FC in name alone, just as Wimbledon were when they moved to Milton Keynes. While they began to get a bit of a following within Peterlee, the support they'd had within the town had all but disappeared. Sponsors had deserted them, bar a handful of hardcore backers. Casual fans weren't prepared to make a 50-mile round trip to watch a team with no identity.

That Esh Winning game, 12 paying punters, was the nadir off the pitch, despite a 4-1 success on the field which ended a 10-game run without a win.

"It was then we actually began to think in terms of next season, is this actually going to happen?" admitted Bob Wray. "The name of the game was survival."

Out on the pitch, manager Jon King was only just managing to get a team out at times. Begging, borrowing and scraping together a band of players who were happy to make that trip to Peterlee, their expenses just about covered but little more.

King was putting his own money in to keep the club going, ensure he could get a team out. The playing budget in their last season at Filtrona Park had been £700 a week, enough to attract some good players but ultimately not enough to keep the team in Division One.

Out of the town, sponsors deserted Shields in droves and playing in Peterlee, the crowds dwindled. Both outcomes had a drastic effect on finances and the budget was slashed, forcing King to run a team on £300 a week instead.

Success on the pitch that first season was secondary to just keeping the team going, keeping the name of South Shields FC alive.

Having used 65 players the season before, King was reduced to appealing in the local press for players, holding trials and using every inch of the contacts he'd built up over the last 15 years to assemble a side that could hold its own in Division Two.

"I was born and bred in South Shields and me and Gary had said we just had to keep the club alive," said King. "It's a big club with massive history and we just had to keep it alive as we always thought there would be someone in South Tyneside who will come and rescue it. I always thought something would happen.

"If it wasn't for me and all my family being from South Shields, I don't think I would have done it, because it was such a nightmare. But I always felt the responsibility because I'd got us this move to Peterlee, I felt I had to give it a season.

"The lads, the committee, got the ground up to scratch with all the painting and everything. The ground was fantastic, a lovely pitch and we were made to feel really welcome. The people down there were brilliant with us but it was a case of having £300 between 16 lads, it is difficult.

"I didn't take anything, in fact I was putting money in that first season out of my own pocket.

"A lot of lads that we'd had in that first season didn't want to know, some of them were from Newcastle and all we could offer them was £20 or £25 to go all the way down to Peterlee. So basically we lost almost an entire team.

"In pre-season, we had to put on a trial for players at Mortimer School. We put it in the press and it was embarrassing really, having to do that. But we had to try everything and from that trial we actually got a lad, Chris Locke, who proved to be a really good signing for us."

A handful of players had stuck with the club after relegation, including Stephen Ramsey who had joined the Mariners as a 17-

year-old back in 2007 and Barrie Smith, who joined the club a couple of years later.

For others, the lure of staying in Division One, extra money, or just a desire to play closer to home proved stronger than remaining at Shields.

King had a reputation as a wheeler-dealer and he needed all his skills, contacts and persuasive powers to ensure he had a squad at his disposal.

There were some highs but mainly lows on the pitch and after a season of struggle, a 17th-placed finish was about as good as the team could have realistically hoped to achieve.

It had started promisingly, with a couple of draws and an FA Cup win over Colne. Even a 5-1 hammering by rivals Roofing at the end of August didn't dent the confidence too much, and a sensational September saw King guide Shields to three successive league wins, a Durham Challenge Cup victory over Willington and then a brilliant FA Vase triumph at Billingham Town after the first game at Peterlee ended in a thrilling 4-4 draw.

That was to be the high point of the season, though, as a bottom-half struggle ensued while at the top end, Roofing clinched the third promotion spot after Seaham Red Star were deducted three points.

Division Two was won by another Shields, the North version, managed by a certain Graham Fenton in his first job as a No 1 after leaving Blyth Spartans where he'd been player, coach and No 2. They'd romped to the title with 100 points and 31 wins from their 42 games but arguably the hardest of those came at home to the Mariners in November when plucky South Shields were devastated to lose 4-3 in injury time, having played the entire second half with 10 men after goalkeeper Jak Wells was sent off. With no replacement keeper on the bench, the Mariners had used three different players between the sticks - Colin White, Lewis Turnbull and Ramsey - only to concede a 95th-minute winner.

If any game epitomised that first season in Peterlee, it was that one. Chaotic, down on their luck but with big-hearted performances from a team thrown together.

They'd survived that season in the garden of Eden but paradise was still no closer. Despite Phil Thornton's hopes when he'd announced the move to Peterlee, there would be no move back to South Shields for the 2014/15 campaign. Instead, it was time to prepare for another season down the road.

After years of struggle, though, the strain was taking its toll.

"Gary Crutwell rang me and asked me to meet him in the Voyager," revealed King. "He told me that it was probably the last season he was going to do it. I told him that if he went, I went.

"He then told me we had a wage bill of around £100 a week! What can I do with that? £300 was hard enough. But that was all we had, down at Peterlee for a second season the sponsors had mainly all gone, there were only a couple who had stuck with us like Kev Bolam and Northern Threads and Nigel Binnie.

"Gary managed to stretch it to £150. Lee Bell had come in as my No 2 by then and he was great, he got us an extra £50 a week and we got the team all kitted out. Then I was sticking about £80 a week in out of my own money so we were up to about £280, and to be fair to Gary, I'd told him I wanted to keep Barrie Smith so he said he'd pay for him out of his own pocket.

"It wasn't great but it was how it was. We had a meeting with the players, told them how it was and how we understood if they couldn't do it. What we did have, though, was great crack, a real togetherness. We asked the players to buy into it. The lads got £200 at Christmas and £200 at the end of the season."

The start of the 2014/15 season, much like the one that preceded it, was good. After winning just once in their opening six Division Two games, a 4-0 thumping of Brandon in which striker David Malloy (whose wages were covered by a sponsorship deal) bagged a hat-trick, Shields went on another good run, winning their next six games on the bounce including 6-0 and 5-0 wins over Thornaby and Tow Law Town in successive games at Eden Lane.

Again, though, that September rain of goals was a false dawn and the onset of winter brought poor results and more difficulties on and off the field.

Players came and went - top scorer Malloy being a significant loss - and King was forced to shuffle his pack, seek further reinforcements and dip into his own pocket again.

"We were never going to get relegated, we always fluctuated

between 10th and 14th. But with £300 a week you can't compete, especially when you had the likes of Seaham Red Star with £1500.

"After 12 games we were top of the league on that budget but when the sticky period came and lads weren't getting paid, it became difficult. Players were having to pay their own fines - if they got a yellow card the club wouldn't pay.

"Gary Crutwell always used to ring on a Friday night to see how we were for the next day. I was regularly saying 'Creets, we've only got 10 players'. So I started having to put more of my own money in, getting players like Sean Sweeney, telling him I'd give him £30 if he came and played, so my £80 was sometimes £110. I never wanted to have the embarrassment of only having 10 players. I think about 10 times we only had 11 players, or 11 plus a sub. Gus Di Lella, who I'd brought in as coach, was playing, Brian Rowe was playing in his 40s.

"It was almost like a Sunday morning side at times but we tried to keep it as professional as possible. They all had training kit, we trained once a week even though sometimes the lads had to pay a couple of quid each. It was a good time but a hard time.

"We knew it was mine and Gary's last season. Lee Bell found it tough after Christmas, he was travelling from Westerhope to Peterlee and picking a few lads up on the way, sometimes not getting back in til after 11pm once he'd dropped players off, so I lost another assistant manager.

"I'm a positive person and I kept people up as best as I could. I never thought about jacking it in. It was our last season, myself and Gary, but if he'd come back and said he'd give it one more go, I'd have done it too.

"We were always waiting on this fella coming in. The amount of times Gary had a businessman hopefully coming in, looking to get Filtrona Park back, only for it to get so far down the line and then the goalposts were moved."

Shields finished the season in 15th spot, boosted by winning their last four games to end the campaign on a high on the pitch.

Off it, already known to a select few, things were about to get even better.

CHAPTER FOUR

May 15, 2015...

A man in his fifties poses for the cameras in front of a clubhouse that has seen better days. He turns, wanders across the football pitch and leans against a goalpost, the cameras clicking again.

There's only a handful of onlookers to the scene on what was to become an iconic day in South Shields FC's history.

The gentleman beams with pride and delight. He runs his hand through a mane of swept-back greying hair which still has large swathes of blond running through it. Along with the piercing blue eyes, he has a look of Michael Douglas about him.

It's the start of a Hollywood story that even the great film actor couldn't have scripted.

There are a few slightly differing tales of how Geoff Thompson came to get involved in South Shields FC but there is no doubt the story starts with a humble begging letter and a proposal to sponsor a stand. Bob Wray, in his commercial manager guise, had spotted an article in the Shields Gazette about Utilitywise, this fast-growing South Shields-based business. Never shy of asking a question, he sent Thompson a letter asking if he'd be interested in any sponsorship opportunities.

"I'd never heard of this company Utilitywise, but I was always on the lookout for new possibilities. I wrote the letter, asked my wife to proof-read it and I'll always remember she said I could charm the birds out of the trees."

It was to be arguably the most important letter ever sent out on the club's behalf.

Utilitywise, an energy consulting firm, were by now one of the largest companies in the region, having only been founded in 2006 by Thompson and his eldest son Adam. A credit card, an overdraft and they were off, growing from three people that year to employing more than 1000 and serving 230,000 customers just nine years later.

By then, Thompson was chief executive, hands-on but with a will to get into other ventures. An encounter with friend Andy Pilley, the founder of another energy supplying business, BES Utilities, whetted his appetite further for football. Pilley, the chairman and owner of Fleetwood Town, had overseen a meteoric rise through the divisions for tiny Fleetwood as they propelled themselves from the North West Counties League to League One of the Football League in less than 10 seasons.

It was a success story that intrigued Thompson, as did the emergence of FC United of Manchester, the club founded by a breakaway group of Manchester United fans bitterly opposed to the takeover of the club by American Malcolm Glazer and disgruntled by the perceived increased commercialism of Premier League football. When Thompson had sat on the judging panel of the Entrepreneur of the Year awards, on the shortlist was Andy Walsh, one of the founders of FC United who as general manager had not only helped create a unique, fan-owned club but had seen them rise through the leagues and move into a new £6.3million stadium within a decade.

The success of Walsh and Pilley resonated with Thompson, a keen football fan himself. A season ticket holder at Sunderland, he had vivid memories of attending games at South Shields' old Simonside Hall ground as a 10-year-old before that famous old ground bit the dust.

Bob Wray's letter revived those memories and set in motion a chain of events which was to culminate in a joyous homecoming.

That missive landed on Thompson's desk not a moment too soon. The club was on the brink of extinction and while there was always a will to continue, the energy among those people responsible for ensuring its survival was on the wane. Gary Crutwell was drained. He'd used up all of his annual leave the year before trying to sort out a new ground, holding meetings with council leaders and backers and the club was no further forward. It's no exaggeration to say that had Geoff Thompson not got involved at that exact moment, there wouldn't be a club today.

"The initial contact we had with Geoff was over a stand sponsorship in memory of his uncle, who used to take him to the games at Simonside Hall," Crutwell said. "Geoff found out via a letterhead or the website that the club was based in Peterlee so he got in touch, asked to meet up and asked if he could get involved.

"There was basically just a few of us keeping the club going and you couldn't have enough people on board."

Thompson insists that despite his encounters with football entrepreneurs elsewhere, he never set out to buy a club, a ground or end up investing so much time and resource into the Mariners. Moreso, it was his passion for the town - and an innate thirst for success and achievement honed in his formative years in South Tyneside - that drove his ambition initially to help get the football club back home.

Born in South Shields in the early 1960s, Thompson wasn't an academic high-flier in the truest sense of the phrase, but realised the importance of education after he'd left Jarrow Grammar School aged 16. From there, he did an engineering apprenticeship with Burgess Industrial Silencers, ironically located on Shaftesbury Avenue. Little did he realise then that almost 40 years later his life would turn full circle and he'd be back on that same road, making more of an impression than he did at Burgess.

His initial stint on Shaftesbury Avenue didn't last long; he took the first of several big decisions to give up his apprenticeship and enrolled at Sunderland Polytechnic to study a four-year sandwich course and gain a combined science degree despite having no A Levels.

"I was self-motivated and, having left a job, got into university without the right qualifications. I thought, 'I've really got to put my back into this'.

"I didn't want to end up flunking this degree because having given up on my apprenticeship route I'd have been in a bit of a pickle had that gone wrong.

"Through sheer hard work and perspiration, and probably less through any academic ability, I got a first.

"I was always quite driven. I had a great childhood and a great upbringing but we weren't a wealthy family. I remember playing golf as a young lad and if I wanted some new golf balls there was no way I'd even think of going to my mam and asking for a few quid.

"I'd get on my bike with a carrier bag and go and spend the afternoon looking for golf balls in the rough. It's that kind of experience that maybe drove me a bit. I don't mean that I was underprivileged, I just thought that if I was going to do well the only way was to work hard."

That work ethic, coupled with his degree, led to a job at British Steel in Redcar, before tired of working shifts, he joined the technical team at Corning Glass in Sunderland, doing a post-graduate diploma and MBA at Newcastle.

Roles at several big companies followed before, in 2003, he was left without a job when Mailcom, the business he'd been managing director at, was sold. Thompson had failed in a management buy-out bid and was left out on his ear.

In his next role, as MD at dabs.com, an IT and Technology sales company, he again grew the business until it was taken over by BT and again he found himself out of a job.

"Persistence and hard work creates your own luck is advice I now give to younger people," he explained in a 2012 interview with The Journal. "It certainly helped drive me forward after each setback. Frustratingly, I had done a good job in each company but my lack of equity or funding meant I was unable to take them to the next stage.

"I had gained a great deal of knowledge and wisdom with each company, but I realised I needed to ensure that I had equity in my next business venture if I was going to be successful."

And successful he certainly was. When Utilitywise was floated on the stock market, Thompson had made his fortune. He was now chief executive of his own multi-million pound company, a revered and respected business leader across the region.

Bob Wray may not have heard about Utilitywise when he wrote that letter, but industry chiefs and local government officials certainly had, and it was this influence and profile that Thompson felt could aid the football club in its hour of need.

"I'm a Shields lad by birth and education. I'm a local bloke and I'm passionate about the area, my hometown and football in general.

"I laugh about about the letter from Bob Wray now and joke that the moral of the story is 'don't reply to these letters'. I thought at the time it was just a request for some sponsorship and I assumed the club was still in Shields but after I met Bob and Gary I was shocked and horrified to hear the tale.

"I said I would try and help and at the time it was just to see if I could assist or influence the search for a new ground back in Shields. I met a number of people, talked to the council and tried to evaluate a number of the options that were available to us but unfortunately they were very few, if none.

"We went down and had a look at Gypsies Green and you could romanticise about that as a location, on the sea front and with that history for the town. It could be argued there were a lot of positives but there was huge cost involved in developing it."

All roads led back to Filtrona Park. By now, John Rundle had provisionally agreed a deal with a container business in Teesside to sell the land to them. The clock was ticking.

Thompson held several meetings with Rundle and even went down to Middlesbrough to meet with the business who planned on buying the ground. He discovered they didn't have planning permission for a container park and suddenly there was a chink of light at the end of the tunnel. Thompson knew he had to move fast, however. The football club were almost out of options but the arch dealmaker, the businessman who had bounced back from numerous setbacks over the years, refused to give up. He had one last play to make.

"I went back to John Rundle and said he could either be remembered as the man who sold me the ground so we could bring our hometown club back to Shields, or he could be remembered as the bloke who allowed a container park to be built on the football ground. It sounds harsh, but I wanted to appeal to his emotional side as someone who had done so much for the football club over the years.

"To his credit, he thought about it for 24 hours and rang me back and we did the deal in no time at all.

"I didn't set out to do that but it ended up being the only choice we had. We had to find a way to get the club back here, and do so quickly before the container company went through the planning process, spent more money on legal and professional fees which would have made the deal more difficult for them to backtrack. It was a moment in time where we had to do that deal or we wouldn't have got back here. The options elsewhere were pretty limited to non-existent.

"When I first got that letter, I had no assumption about being chairman or going on the journey we've been on. It was purely about getting the club back into the town. It was all about listening to the predicament the club was in, given my South Shields and South Tyneside background. Listening to the plight of the club, I just felt it was the right thing to do, to try and help."

The cameras are finished clicking, Thompson is finished posing for pictures. A statement is drafted announcing the return of South Shields FC to Filtrona Park after the businessman's deal has been completed. Only it's not Filtrona Park any longer, renamed instead as Mariners Park in homage to the club's nickname.

There are further changes. Thompson is announced as the club's new chairman, taking over from Gary Crutwell who steps down to vice-chairman. It's the start of a reshuffle off the pitch, which will see a board of directors appointed, including Thompson's daughter Stephanie Smith, and his long-time business associate Michael Orr, handed the role of managing director.

They will play key roles in the development of the club off the pitch. Thompson wants to move quickly, up through the leagues and push for National League status. There is a budget in place to strengthen the team and plans afoot to transform the clubhouse with a quick, but costly, refurbishment of the bar areas upstairs and downstairs.

This isn't just about celebrating a return to their old home and resting on their laurels. Bigger and better is the aim. The pace of change takes Crutwell and other old-stagers by surprise as the ground they had known so well for two decades evolves before they've had time to draw breath.

It's a revamp that is quickly matched by the metamorphosis of the playing squad. The revolution is under way.

CHAPTER FIVE

SEPTEMBER 4, 2015...

Jon King proudly poses for a picture with his latest signing as his South Shields revolution starts to gather pace.

In the three months since Geoff Thompson's arrival as chairman, it has been almost a revolving door at Mariners Park as new player after new player are unveiled. It's a busy time for King and for media man Dan Prince. Every week seemed to bring a new announcement.

Some big names on the South Tyneside football scene had already been recruited. Ex-skipper Leepaul Scroggins had returned to his hometown club from Shildon, as had Jonny Wightman, this time from Dunston UTS. The highest-profile signing, though, had been David Foley, a fantastic piece of business ensuring the talented former Hartlepool United and Fort Lauderdale attacker was now easily the best and most well-known player operating in the Northern League Division Two.

Until now, that is.

If Foley's capture had caused a stir, it was nothing compared to the man who put pen to paper in the first week of September. Julio Andres Arca.

It was a signing that would not only capture the imagination of the South Shields public, but also sparked headlines on a far wider basis. King was later to call it the "greatest Northern League signing ever".

It's hard to argue against it.

SOUTH SHIELDS HAD STARTED life under Thompson with great optimism.

What the new chairman had promised was the means and funds to deliver immediate success on the pitch, with promotion the only real aim for that season.

Having finished 17th in May, it was evident that a completely new squad would need to be assembled if a top-three finish was to be achieved and King, with his vast array of contacts and a confidence that he could sell snow to eskimos, was in his element now that he had a bumper kitty with which to back up his verbal promises.

King's infectiousness and drive meant he was perfect for the role. In the early 1990s, I'd spent several weekends in his company as we travelled down to Notts County as schoolboy footballers, playing games for their youth teams as we tried to forge careers in the game. I was painfully shy at the time, but King was the polar opposite: brash and loud with a confidence that bordered on arrogance at times, many of the key traits that you needed to make it in the pro game.

Twenty five years on, that confidence and self-belief was still there. He needed it, too. For all that there was a healthy budget to work with, King still had to sell players the project at South Shields, convince them to drop down a level or two when they were getting bigger and better offers to continue playing in Northern League Division One or even the Evo-Stik League.

He tackled it with gusto and joy. Having been forced to scrap around for players the season previous, putting in his own money at times just to keep the budget respectable, he could now target a better calibre of player.

What King was determined to do, however, was bring the right characters to the club, not just players motivated by money.

"The first two signings I brought in, Jonny Wightman and

Leepaul Scroggins, were easy because they wanted to play for Shields. It's a domino effect, once you've got them in others want to come. David Foley was a huge signing and then after that, it became easy, especially with the start we had. It was just a great place to be.

"I was buzzing. When you go from training at Bents Park and struggling to find 11 players to having a wage bill of £3000 a week - and we could have had more if we wanted. When I met a player and sat him down, they could feed off how excited I was.

"The players I was bringing in were great, there was a signing every week, big signings, whether it was Daryll Hall coming back, Leepaul Scroggins, Jonny Wightman.

"I wanted to get captains in. When you've got money, you can attract horrible people. Every manager can make bad signings but if you look at the players I brought in from that day, I don't think I made many bad signings. They were all lads I knew and not only were they fantastic footballers, they were all leaders.

"We signed a great left-back, Adam Curry, who ended up going to Hull City. There was Michael Turner who we got in the from Peterlee days, Daryl Hall, Ben Riding who we got in down the Peterlee days. We knew at this point towards the end of the Peterlee season that we were going back to Mariners Park and we knew we had big money. We met Ben, told him the crack and he was good enough to trust us and he signed on that.

"It was a great side, a team of real winners and we went on to set records."

It hadn't started positively, however.

The first game of the campaign was back at Mariners Park as Northallerton were the visitors on a buoyant day in which 417 fans came through the turnstiles to welcome the club back to the town.

Northallerton, however, hadn't read the script and the party soon turned flat when the visitors raced into a three-goal lead after just 32 minutes. Shields' cause wasn't helped by Scroggins missing a penalty, and while they valiantly fought back with goals from Lee Scott and an injury-time Foley strike, it wasn't enough to get the new era off to a winning start.

The disjointed nature of that first game should, in hindsight, have come as no surprise. In total, there were 20 new players who came through the door that summer and 10 of them took to the field at some point against Northallerton, with Barrie Smith the only survivor from the Peterlee days in the starting line-up.

Scroggins, Hall, Wightman, Foley and Curry were joined in the summer by several other big names. Lewis Galpin, a highly-rated 21-year-old defender, joined from West Auckland where he'd formed a partnership in the middle of the back four with Hall, while talented left-winger Wayne Phillips switched from rivals Jarrow Roofing to make Shields the next stop in a stellar non-league journey which had seen him win the FA Vase with Spennymoor and play for Gateshead, Blyth Spartans and Whitley Bay.

Robert Briggs was persuaded to drop two divisions and leave Spennymoor Town to return to the club where he'd began his Northern League career as a teenager. Along with Phillips and Foley, they were three signings who would end up taking the club all the way from Division Two to Wembley.

Warren Byrne brought guaranteed goals, having fired Newton Aycliffe and Seaham Red Star to Division Two promotion in a long career that also saw him star for Gateshead, Spennymoor and Bishop Auckland, among others, while another forward, Lee Scott, came with Division Two experience.

The most experienced signing of all was Wayne Buchanan, a defender who played professionally at Bolton Wanderers, Chesterfield, in Australia and had captained Irish side Lisburn Distillery in the Europa League.

One thing most of the players had, also, was an affinity to the club or the area. Scroggins, leader and midfield inspiration during Gary Steadman's time in charge, and attacker Wightman were South Shields lads and had played for the club before, as had Hall and Gilberto Chapim. Foley and Curry were Sand Dancers; Galpin had been born in Shields and now lived in Hebburn while Phillips had been living in the town for the last 15 years. Another South Tynesider, Lee McMahon, swapped the captaincy at neighbours Hebburn to join the Mariners while striker Aris Lokonga Guerin had lived in Shields and played for Roofing.

Several goalkeepers were brought in as King tried to find a No 1 he was happy with. Gareth Young, Steve Hubery, Dale Connor and Ryan Beal arrived before the season started before Scott Pocklington signed at the beginning of September from Bishop Auckland. Midfielders Kenny Ball and Adam Sakr were also added to the ranks, illustrating the huge turnover of players, with just Smith, Ramsey, Turner and Riding remaining from the previous campaign.

Pre-season had been a huge success. The return to the town had captured the imagination, with fans flocking through the gates to watch Shields take on some strong sides. Darlington provided the opposition for the first game back at Mariners Park, guaranteeing a big crowd, while Spennymoor sent a side and FA Vase holders North Shields made the trip through the Tyne Tunnel, only to make the return journey on the back of a 1-0 defeat.

They were one of three Division One sides that the Mariners defeated in pre-season, and while results in friendlies are never a true indicator of what a season will be like, it justified South Shields' tag as favourites for the Division Two title.

With less than 15 minutes to go of their second league game of the season, that moniker looked undeserved.

On the back of the Northallerton defeat, King had made several changes to his team for the following game against Billingham Town. With so many options at his disposal, he had to find the right blend but with 78 minutes on the clock, Shields trailed 2-0 and looked set to open the season with two defeats.

Had they done so, who knows how the season may have panned out? It's debatable whether it would have made much difference; Shields had that much quality and firepower in their squad that it was obvious that once they gelled, they would put most teams to the sword and so it proved in a stunning last 12 minutes that sent the home fans away happy. Scroggins and Byrne levelled the scores then with just a minute left on the clock, Foley showed his class with a brilliant left-footed volley that screamed into the net to hand Shields three points which had looked unlikely just a quarter of an hour earlier.

Shields were off and running. A 6-0 demolition of Darlington RA was followed by a 2-1 win over Heaton Stannington as the first four games of the season were all played at home. The first away trip of the season was to Willington, and ended with a 4-1 victory, before the run of wins was halted by a disappointing 2-2 draw at Alnwick.

Shields' bid to bounce straight back to winning ways lasted just two minutes at home to Ryhope CW when the game was abandoned after an injury to Sakr following a collision with the away team's goalkeeper, an incident that fortunately wasn't as bad as first feared thanks in part to the quick medical attention from physio Andy Morris, another summer recruit to the staff.

A Bank Holiday Monday win at neighbours Hebburn Town meant Shields ended August on top of the table, a position they didn't concede for the remainder of the season. Indeed the defeat in their next outing, at home to Easington Colliery, was to be their last reverse until January as an incredible 21-game unbeaten run set records and established Shields as not only the best side in Division Two, but also a force to be reckoned with across the Northern League.

That it also coincided with a certain Argentinian's arrival did not just make people in the North East sit up and take notice of what was happening in South Shields, but put them back on the footballing map on a global level.

―――

WHEN PETER REID splashed out £3.5million to bring Julio Arca to Sunderland in 2000, it began an unlikely love affair with the region that two decades later is still as passionate as ever.

From being unable to speak a word of English on his arrival, Arca became the city's adopted son, their most-loved foreign import since Nissan's arrival 16 years earlier. Even a five-year spell at rivals Middlesbrough didn't tarnish his reputation among Black Cats fans who loved his all-action style, quick feet and magical left peg.

Arca was just 19 years of age when Reid brought him 7,000 miles across the world. Arca was swapping Buenos Aires for Wearside, having been spotted by Reid playing for Argentina's Under-21s against England in the summer of 2000. Sunderland had just finished seventh in the Premier league for the second season in succession and Reid was keen to maintain the club's position in the upper echelons of the top flight.

The success didn't last, but Arca's reputation among the fans did. A goal on his debut against West Ham United helped his cause no end and he was successfully converted from a left-back into a midfielder by Reid. He couldn't stop Sunderland being relegated in his second season with the club, but was a star performer as they bounced back to the top flight under Mick McCarthy, his hardwork, commitment, desire and ability delighting fans and pundits alike as he was named in the 2005 Championship team of the year.

In the summer of 2006, with Sunderland back in the Championship after just one season in the Premier League, Arca swapped Wearside for Teesside, making the short trip down the A19 to become Gareth Southgate's first signing as Middlesbrough manager in a £1.75million deal. It ended a six-year spell at Sunderland and started another chapter of his career as he went on to become a fan favourite at Boro too, earning the captain's armband and being named Supporters' and Players' Player of the Season in 2011.

Within a couple of years, however, the glittering professional career was over. A long-standing toe injury forced him to retire in 2014, aged just 32, and that seemed to be that for a cult hero on both Wearside and Teesside.

Arca, however, couldn't keep away from the game and was persuaded to have a few games for a Sunday morning side, Willow Pond FC, by one of his friends. The story made headlines all over the world and King, a huge Sunderland fan, had an idea.

King approached Arca to see if he'd be interested in South Shields and invited him down to Mariners Park for a chat and to watch a couple of games. The Argentinian, seeing the potential of the club and having been bitten by the football bug again, was keen to get involved.

Negotiations proved to be a little trickier, with a playing budget to work within, until the club came up with a solution whereby Arca wouldn't get a weekly wage, but instead would receive a percentage of the gate receipts.

While Arca had only played a handful of Sunday morning games in the last couple of years, King knew it was a gamble worth taking.

"I hadn't seen Julio play for a couple of years but it was a no-brainer. He was telling me he was fit and I knew how big a signing he would be.

"Anything I asked for, I got. Geoff and Mike Orr, Geoff's right-hand man, were great with me. So when I asked about Julio, Geoff said to go for it.

"We knew Julio would bring more people in, we would sell more merchandise, lager, programmes, all of that. It was a no-brainer.

"The club got a fantastic deal, just look what he's done for them. No one will ever make a signing like that again, it's like Newcastle Benfield signing Alan Shearer. He was a legend at Sunderland, like Kevin Phillips."

King was to later try and sign Shola Ameobi after his release from Newcastle United, but couldn't pull that deal off, but even if the Nigerian international had arrived at Mariners Park, it is doubtful whether he'd have had the impact Arca did. The midfielder made his debut against Stokesley SC two days after his signing and his impact, as King predicted, was immediate, both on and off the pitch.

In some ways, it was a disappointing afternoon for the Mariners. Up against the division's bottom side, who had lost every game up until then, Shields were expected to comfortably win, especially given they had two ex-Premier League footballers in their team with Arca joined by another former Sunderland player, striker Ryan Noble, who had made his debut the previous week against Easington. Noble, still only 23, had played five times for Sunderland's first-team after making a name for himself as one of the club's hottest prospects at youth and reserve team level, but drifted down the leagues after being released by the Black Cats. Whereas Arca was to become a legend at Shields, as he was at Sunderland, Noble lasted just two games and by the time he was 25 had disappeared from football completely.

Arca was here to stay, though. The script seemed written as with Shields struggling to break down a resolute Stokesley defence who were belying their previous results, Arca eventually broke the deadlock with a debut goal to the delight of the large crowd at Mariners Park.

The party was spoiled, again however, late on, as Joshua Chambers equalised against the run of play and despite late pressure, Arca's debut ended in a disappointing 1-1 draw.

If it had been a let-down on the pitch, there was a huge bonus off it. A crowd of 764 - the largest in years for a home game at South Shields - had come through the turnstiles to watch the game as the 'Julio effect' had an instant impact. Seven days earlier, 642 had watched the Mariners in action against Easington. Attendances were on the march. The first home game of the season against Northallerton had been watched by 417 while 243 had come through the gate for the 6-0 demolition of Darlington RA.

Arca's deal, whereby he received a percentage of the gate, was proving to be a masterstroke.

CHAPTER SIX

The rest of 2015 saw Shields obliterate all before them.

They won 13 league games in a row, including a 9-1 demolition of Tow Law Town on November 14 in front of a crowd of 1,412 - a Northern League Division Two record. It was a stunning performance and a stunning turn-out from the South Tyneside public as the Mariners recorded a bigger attendance than some National League and League Two clubs. Shields were helped by the international break in the football calendar which meant neither Newcastle United nor Sunderland had games that day and they picked the perfect afternoon to produce their best performance of the season.

It would prove to be another pivotal moment in the club's history, as Newcastle and Sunderland fans - many disenchanted with the way their clubs were being run - saw the standard of football on their doorsteps.

Arca was undoubtedly the big draw, especially among SAFC supporters who wanted to see their former hero in action again, but the community feel, fantastic football and affordability that Shields could provide undoubtedly helped too. Many fans who had watched the Mariners for the first time were to ultimately return, some quitting their season tickets at the Premier League duo to start following South Shields.

Shields were riding high at the top of the Division Two table, and had also progressed in the knockout competitions. Crook Town and Chester-le-Street had been defeated in the Durham Challenge Cup and two rounds of the League Cup had also been negotiated. The big one remained the FA Vase, though, and wins over Washington and Bishop Auckland had set up a tough tie at Division One high-fliers Consett on their new 3G pitch. Arca was forced off early but his replacement, Sakr, got the only goal deep into extra time to seal their passage through to the next round.

It set up a huge clash against Morpeth Town in the next round, a game which was to have repercussions much further down the line. The tie was scheduled for December 12 at Mariners Park but didn't eventually get played until January 20, 2016 - back up at Consett - after a series of postponements due to the weather. Seven times the game was called off, with Shields officials unhappy with the referee's judgement on at least one occasion, and the Football Association eventually ruled the game should be switched to a neutral venue, with Belle View Park hosting the game.

Even that didn't initially go to plan, with snow and frost scuppering the first attempt but finally the tie took place, and what a stunner it was. Nothing could separate the two teams after 120 minutes of absorbing, end-to-end football and with the scores tied at 3-3, the game went to penalties.

It looked at one stage as if the tie might go on all night as the two sets of players swapped successful kicks, but ultimately it was Morpeth who went through 10-9 on penalties after a sudden death shoot-out which saw Riding miss the chance to win the game for Shields before Scroggins agonisingly saw his kick saved by Karl Dryden.

It was the end of the road for Shields, but it had given them a taste for the Vase. They could only watch on as Morpeth went from strength to strength after that win, finishing up at Wembley. It would be another 12 months before the Mariners would emulate them - and it was only just the beginning of an FA Vase relationship with the Highwaymen that would end in even more controversy.

January was to be a blip in the season. The 20-game winning run ended, the Vase exit was followed by Shields losing both of their league games that month, defeated 3-2 by title rivals Ryhope CW and then 1-0 at Billingham Synthonia. It was a blow to the Mariners' promotion hopes, especially given the further investment they'd made in the squad since the season had started. Another South Tyneside native, defender Ibby Hassan, had joined after seven years with Whitby Town while Dunston's FA Vase hero Andrew Bulford and fellow striker Lewis Teasdale had joined to boost the firepower. John Grey had joined from North Shields as King set about ensuring he had enough resources at his disposal, with Shields still chasing silverware on four fronts.

Hassan and Teasdale played key roles as Shields bounced back to winning ways in one of those competitions as they stunned the pros of Gateshead by beating them 3-2 to reach the semi-finals of the Durham Challenge Cup. Teasdale scored a second-half winner to see off their rivals in another game which profiled not only the rise of the team on the pitch, but also illustrated the potential off it with almost 650 people watching on a bitterly cold Tuesday night.

The conditions weren't as bad as those both sides faced a couple of weeks later, however, when Shields saw off neighbours Hebburn Town 5-2 in the Ernest Armstrong Memorial Cup. With the pitch cutting up amid driving rain, an entertaining game saw Martyn Coleman score twice on his debut after joining from Penrith, where he had built up a reputation as one of the Northern League's most prolific marksmen.

Coleman's arrival showed how players were prepared now to travel far and wide to join the Shields bandwagon, tempted by the ambition of the club and the money they could now offer. Coleman's journeys from Cumbria a couple of times a week were never likely to last, but he made a big impact in his short time at the club as replacement for Bulford, who left to join Ashington after six goals in 15 appearances.

Shields' participation in the Ernest Armstrong Cup - competed exclusively for by Division Two sides - ended at the next stage as Billingham Synthonia beat them 2-1, and when on March 1 they lost their Durham Challenge Cup semi-final to Newton Aycliffe on penalties, they had been defeated five times in the 12 games they'd played in 2016, albeit two had come via penalty shoot-outs against Division One sides.

The league campaign, however, remained well on course and after the defeat to Synners, Shields won the next nine Division Two fixtures on the bounce to extend their lead at the top of the table. Included in that run was a 5-0 home success over Crook Town in which top scorer Warren Byrne continued his rich vein of form with a stunning overhead kick - his second that month after another gloriously-acrobatic effort against Esh Winning - that had the Shields website purring that it was a "true goal of the season contender". They were to be premature with their prediction.

By now, the Mariners had been left to focus solely on promotion. The final hope of reaching a cup final had ended with defeat against North Shields in the League Cup, watched by more than 1,300 fans at Mariners Park. It was a staggering attendance for a Tuesday night game, illustrating further the pull of two historic sides who were on the up, but for once the home team couldn't rise to the occasion and were 3-0 down after 34 minutes and never recovered from that poor start as the FA Vase holders cruised to victory.

"We wanted to give them better than that," said King of the defeat. "We were disappointing. We let ourselves down. But our remit at the start of the season was always to win promotion."

The one bright spot from the evening was that Ryhope, in league action, had lost 4-2 against Easington Colliery, meaning Shields were eight points clear of the third-placed side and six better off than second-placed Synthonia, with two games in hand.

Promotion was in their hands. A rare defeat against Heaton Stannington was followed by a run of three games in five days that were ultimately to end in celebration. First up, Shields atoned for their disappointing draw at home to Stokesley earlier in the season by beating the division's bottom side 3-0, then followed it up with a 3-1 home win over Brandon United to put them on the verge of the top flight.

Promotion was sealed on a memorable night 48 hours later. The trip to Easington Colliery almost mirrored the distance Shields used to travel to Peterlee, but whereas they had struggled for supporters in those days, this time they were backed by several hundred fans eager to be part of the party. In the shadows of Eden Lane, it was fitting that one of the players who had been part of those struggles, Michael Turner, should score the goal that sent the club back into Division One with a fine header from a superb Briggs corner.

The reaction among the travelling hordes was jubilant and when the final whistle sounded, the players joined them in celebrating an achievement that the club could barely have dreamed of 12 months ago. A year to the day after 68 people had watched them struggle to a goalless draw against Billingham Town, more than 400 cheered them back into the top flight.

"Without Geoff, we could never have done this," said King. "But also, all of the people who kept the club alive. Without those people, Geoff Thompson could never have come into the club. This is for all of those committee members and also for all of those fans."

King wasn't content with just promotion, however, and demanded the players achieve two more goals before the season was out - the title and 100 points.

They achieved both in the same game, a 4-0 win at Crook Town which confirmed the championship crown with two games remaining and broke the century point barrier in the process. Crook's old ground, Millfield, is steeped in history. One of the most famous venues in the Northern League, it was bought by Crook Town in 1989 for £685 and had witnessed some remarkable occasions, including 17,500 cramming into the ground to watch their FA Amateur Cup tie against Walton and Hersham in 1952, one of several games that saw five-figure crowds at Millfield.

Times had become tougher over the last few years and the old ground hadn't seen scenes like they did when Shields came to town for a long while. The huge main stand, built in 1926 for £,1,300, housed hundreds of Sand Dancers as they celebrated on four occasions during the 90 minutes, then for another 10 minutes out on the pitch along with the players, doused in bubbly and singing songs about Arca, Thompson and more.

The revelry had started just four minutes in when Daryll Hall's header put Shields ahead.

Arca, fittingly, was to have a say too. Gracing the turf that many famous names had played on before him, he showed his class by pulling the strings from the centre of midfield before coolly adding a second goal before half-time from the penalty spot.

The win, and title, were secured after the break as Teasdale also scored from the spot after Byrne had rolled home his 30th of the season to continue a magical spell of form from the prolific striker.

A couple of weeks earlier, Byrne had sprung to national prominence after footage of his stunning goal against Tow Law Town went viral on Twitter and Facebook. Two days after clinching promotion against Easington in a game he sat on the bench for, Byrne took his frustrations out on the Lawyers with an incredible strike put him on the world map. Lurking just outside the penalty box, Byrne first controlled a headed clearance with his right foot, then flicked it over his head before swivelling and unleashing a dipping left-foot volley into the net.

Media man Dan Prince recognised the stunning nature of the goal and quickly posted it online. Social media went mad for the net-buster. Clips of it were posted and re-posted around the world and the goal was viewed more than 3.5million times on YouTube. USA news channel CNN chose it as one of their goals of the week, Byrne was invited onto Sky Sports show Soccer AM, while England and Spurs star Dele Alli congratulated the 34-year-old on his strike. The goal was eventually named as Budweiser's Dream Goal of 2016, chosen by ex-England internationals Jamie Carragher and Jamie Redknapp, winning the football club £50,000 in prize money.

It marked an incredible end to an unforgettable 12 months for the club. The Division Two championship trophy was presented to captain Leepaul Scroggins after the 5-1 home win over Willington, in front of more than a 1,000 fans who braved the wet and wind, and a floodlight failure that delayed the start of the second half by 15 minutes.

It wasn't to be the last time the floodlights were to play a key role on a huge day for the club, but for now, the darkness had been lifted and South Shields FC was once again bathed in light. The town was on a high, attendances were regularly topping four figures and the club was back on the footballing map.

"The dressing room was brilliant," said King. "I made sure that when we had 1,500 people at games, when we had 500 people following us to places like Chester-le-Street, that the lads spent time with the fans. The fans like to see the players in the bar afterwards, have a pint with them, talk about the game and I made sure that happened.

"We had such a good squad. I brought in the likes of Martyn Coleman, David Foley, Wayne Phillips, Danny Carson, excellent signings. There were lads there who had seen us through the tough times as well, like Barrie Smith and Ramma.

"Getting Julio Arca was brilliant. I knew it would be big but it wasn't just down to Julio, it was down to the team, winning 20-odd games, the performances of players, beating First Division teams in the Vase. Everybody was behind us.

"When we won the Second Division, Geoff was in the dressing room, getting covered in champagne, and he said 'Jon, we're going to get our hometown team through the pyramid' and I'd joked about getting a statue of him outside the ground. We had a great relationship."

CHAPTER SEVEN

SEPTEMBER 4, 2016...

The phone rings in the King household and Jon, still enjoying a lazy Sunday morning, picks it up.

It's Geoff Thompson, requesting that he meet him at Mariners Park for a chat. It was to be a meeting that changed everything.

Less than 24 hours earlier, South Shields had seen off a youthful Whitley Bay side 4-2 to make it four wins on the bounce. Still in the early throes of the new season, the Mariners were recovering from a disappointing start to finally find the form their huge summer outlay and recruitment demanded.

That victory had put Shields third in the Division One standings, level on points with leaders and defending champions Shildon, but with an inferior goal difference. More than 1400 fans had packed into Mariners Park on Non-League Day, taking advantage of a weekend with no Premier League football to watch a vibrant, entertaining affair that saw three second-half goals from the home side see off a Whitley side that had led 2-1 at half-time.

It was the second time inside the opening four weeks of the season that the two teams had met. Bay, featuring a young, talented group of players, had held Shields to a 3-3 draw that day as the

Mariners continued their sticky start. It was the first game of the new season and they'd yet to register a win.

Four games, and four wins, later they were flying high. Confidence was back, a new-look team looked to be starting to gel with a 6-0 win away at Chester-le-Street giving optimism that a title challenge may be on the cards after all. All thoughts of the poor start to the campaign seemed to have been forgotten.

Not behind the scenes, it seemed.

King admits he felt uneasy after Thompson's phone call, but buoyed by the victory the day before and with a glance at the league table, put it to the back of his mind. He showered, grabbed something to eat and left his wife Claire and son JJ to head to the ground.

Thompson took him into the main stand, sat him down and delivered the bombshell news that he was no longer the club's manager. Crutwell was pottering below them, sweeping the terraces of the mess created the day before, oblivious that one of his good pals, who he'd worked so closely alongside to keep the club alive in the Peterlee days, had been sacked.

King said: "When Geoff told me he was going to make a change I couldn't believe it. I was in tears, I couldn't get my head around what had happened.

"He told me that nobody knew, only him, Mike Orr and Lee Picton. Gary Crutwell was down in front of us, sweeping the stand, but he didn't know. I told him that I thought it should have gone to the board, I said you're hardly ever here. Obviously he'd put that much money in he could make the decision but I thought it should have went to the board. He's the man though, it's his decision."

A case of the King is dead, long live the King.

The news soon broke, with the club immediately releasing a statement confirming King's departure and thanking him for everything he'd done over five years and 256 games in charge. It was described as an "incredibly difficult decision" and one made with a "heavy heart" by the chairman and board of directors.

The next line of the statement gave some insight into the shock decision. "With the medium to long-term future in mind, the club felt that this course of action was necessary."

The rumour mill started grinding over who would replace King in the dugout. Within an hour of the news breaking, I'd received a call from a prominent non-league manager asking that his name be put forward but when I spoke to Thompson a couple of hours later he seemed disinterested, fuelling the suspicion that he already had someone in mind. He revealed that the decision wasn't results-related or a reaction to the first few games of the campaign. He talked of having agonised over the decision for a period of time and of needing to "strengthen the management" and it quickly became evident that this wasn't a snap judgement call and that there was already a plan in his mind of how he wanted to move forward.

The club statement revealed that assistant manager Picton had been placed in interim charge, but in reality he had been handed the keys by Thompson and told he could bring in someone alongside him. There was only ever going to be one man for the job.

On the other side of the Tyne, Graham Fenton had been carving a reputation as a manager of some repute with North Shields. Having taken over in April 2012, he transformed the fallen giants from a side stuck in Division Two of the Northern League to Wembley winners inside three years, putting into practice all the knowledge and skills he'd acquired from a playing career that had brought him two League Cup winners' medals while with Aston Villa and Leicester City, along with a spell at Blackburn Rovers where he infamously, for Newcastle United fans, scored twice against them in the 1995/96 title race to help deny his boyhood team the Premiership crown.

Crucially, however, once his professional playing days were over and he'd returned to the North East to star for, among others, Blyth Spartans, Fenton's coaching career had led him to Monkseaton High School where he'd helped bring national success to their Academy set-up, in tandem with their head coach: Picton.

Thompson moved quick and once Picton had spoken to his pal to see if he'd be interested, negotiations were quickly concluded, with Fenton resigning as North Shields boss. Just over 24 hours after King's dismissal, he was appointed co-manager of South Shields alongside Picton, who stepped up from his assistant manager role to take joint charge of the helm.

While many queried how joint-managers would work in practice, having worked side by side for so many years at the school, it was a partnership that the duo were confident could be replicated at a more senior level.

For Fenton, it was an obvious move despite the success he'd achieved - and was continuing to produce - on the opposite side of the river.

"I don't think I'm speaking out of turn by saying North Shields had gone as far as it could go. It has no real ambition to progress through the leagues, they went up quite a few years ago and it hit them hard and were another club that nearly went to the wall. They had to reset and did so when they sold Appleby Park, they had to start from scratch again.

"I knew I'd taken the team as far as I could.

"If Lee hadn't come up with the proposal of joining him at South Shields then I possibly would have just carried on until something better had turned up.

"It's difficult when you are working hard and trying to achieve things when you know you are limited. Obviously we have limitations here at South Shields, but nothing near the limitations that were put in front of you at North Shields."

Not that he'd ever admit to feelings of jealousy when casting an eye over what was developing over the water.

"There was no envy." A smile forms across his face. "Don't forget I came here and won 3-0 and that was when the money was starting to be thrown around.

"There was no envy but there was always the case of there being a club which had ambition, which wanted to progress up through the leagues and looking across the Tyne to see what was going on.

"I was just in that frame of mind where I was needing a fresh challenge, I had taken the club as far as I could."

The swiftness of the whole process, however, left a bitter taste in the mouth of some people. Suspicion lingered that this had been planned in advance, concocted by the two friends over many a cuppa at Monkseaton and then presented behind King's back to Thompson and Orr.

Picton, in particular, was cast as the villain of the piece, accused of stabbing King in the back to land his dream job alongside his friend. Social media vitriol dripped from many a keyboard and many a forum comment was posted criticising both him and Thompson.

"At the time, I'm not going to lie, it was unpleasant for me," admits Picton now. "People love conspiracy theories. They love putting two and two together and making five.

"It's drama and a lot of people out there have got their own agenda. It suited some agendas for people to try and drive a story that just wasn't true. At the end of the day, there was one person who made the decision to sack Jon and that was Geoff Thompson and he's the owner of the football club.

"I'd left a role at Blyth Spartans, a club that was three tiers higher, to come and join South Shields. Even looking back and reflecting now, 100 times out of 100 I'd do the same thing.

"I know Jon personally had an issue with me staying on and felt that out of some kind of loyalty I should have gone with him. But I am very serious and I'm very committed. I've sacrificed a lot to get where I am today and I wasn't prepared to just walk away from this football club just because the owner felt that the current manager wasn't up to the task.

"We got beat off Marske in the FA Cup, we then got beat away at Newton Aycliffe, we drew against Consett and drew against Whitley Bay so in the first four games we were winless. It obviously picked up a little bit from there and you'd have to speak to Geoff about the ins and outs of why he actually sacked Jon King."

Thompson is happy to talk on the record about it when we meet up. The passing of time hasn't changed his outlook on the process and while there are some regrets, he is still adamant it was the right thing to do. The only concession he will make is that the timing of the decision could have been better.

"It was incredibly difficult and if anybody says they make those decisions easily, they aren't quite wired right. I agonised over it. I still have contact with Jon and I have the utmost respect for him and what he did, and his passion and loyalty to the club was second to none, so you can imagine how I felt when I had to sit with him and say 'you're doing a great job but if I take a one, two or three-year view, I don't think you're right for the club Jon, over the long-term'.

"The problem I agonised over was when was the right time to make that decision. I could have waited. The fans gave me a right rough ride, and rightly so one could argue, but we had started well so there was nothing on the pitch that suggested it was time to make a change.

"But I felt for the long-term planning, what we were trying to create, it was just about style, behaviour, values, where we wanted to be, how professional we wanted to be. That's not a slight on Jon, I just felt I had to make a call on that at some point and the longer it went on, the more difficult it would become.

"I tried to deliver that decision fairly and compassionately and make sure Jon had as soft a landing as we could. We didn't cut him off at the knees, we paid him for nine months which I didn't have to do. It's a contradiction in terms, you're making a horrible tough decision and you're trying to sweeten it. You're never going to be able to do that so in Jon's eyes he'll still say I made a mistake but he's a very loyal Shields man and he's hopefully come to accept it."

That may be wishful thinking on Thompson's behalf. Time is a great healer and the pain at his dismissal isn't as raw as it once was, but King admits he still struggles to get his head around it all.

"I went to Wembley and I was heartbroken. I was buzzing for the lads, that they'd won, but I was heartbroken. I'd been out the night before in Covent Garden and the fans were great with me but after we'd won it, I was chuffed for the lads but I went back to the hotel as I was bubbling up.

"That could have been me. My mam and dad always said if you do the right things in life you get looked after. I did the right things for that club and I didn't get looked after. I don't want to feel that way but it's how I feel.

"The Peterlee times were dark but we had a togetherness. I have a real sense of pride from that, keeping the club alive. I was a local lad and I just wanted people, my family, to be proud of me.

"But I wanted to get that club into the Football League. I could have got them through the leagues but I wasn't given the chance to finish what I started."

That job now fell to Picton and Fenton. Shields were nicely-placed in the league but needed to show more consistency and raise their standards if they were to achieve a top-two finish, the minimum requirement for the season with promotion to the Evo-Stik North division the main goal. Anything else would be a bonus.

While Thompson may have thought the start to the season was good, the new management duo didn't. They'd already lost once and drawn twice in the league and with Morpeth, Shildon and North Shields all looking strong in the early throes of the campaign, they knew they already couldn't afford too many more slip-ups.

Of equal concern to them was the make-up of the squad. Assembled predominantly by King in the summer, there had been a number of high-profile acquisitions, all of whom had undoubted ability and who had been playing at a higher level in the non-league pyramid.

The capture of Jon Shaw was a huge statement of intent. Recently released by Gateshead, where he had been a full-time pro, Shaw had been persuaded to drop down several rungs to become a part-time player with Shields while developing his coaching career at Middlesbrough. Shaw had made his name as a striker, appearing for boyhood club Sheffield Wednesday as a youngster before enjoying a successful lower league career. He moved to the North East in 2010 to sign for Gateshead where he bagged 45 goals under Ian Bogie's management to earn a big move to Luton Town, returning to the Heed two years later where he again led the attack before being used in a defensive role towards the end of his time at the International Stadium.

"Jon King rang me up and to be honest, I wasn't 100% sure. I had a sit down with Lee and Jon and they were really passionate and explained the project, and it just intrigued me. The opportunity to get in at the ground floor level.

"I was coaching more and more and I thought it was probably time to go part-time. However, I had travelled the country all my career and the lure of playing Northern League football wasn't great. It wasn't a jump I would have taken if it wasn't part of a progression. The club, Geoff included, sold that really well to me."

Still a few months before his 33rd birthday, it was a superb signing for Shields and one that made the rest of the Northern League sit up and take notice, especially when he was joined at Mariners Park by his old Gateshead team-mate Craig Baxter.

Just a couple of years earlier, Baxter had been Gateshead's marauding right-back on their run to the Conference play-off final, where they narrowly missed out on promotion back to the Football League with a 2-1 defeat at Wembley against Cambridge United. Now, also at the end of his Gateshead contract, he too turned down several offers from higher-placed teams to move into part-time football on South Tyneside.

A third ex-Gateshead player joined in the form of Carl Finnigan. The ex-Newcastle youngster's nomadic career had seen him enjoy spells in the Scottish Premier League with Falkirk, St Johnstone and Dundee, along with expeditions to more sunnier climes than Scotland, playing in both South Africa and Botswana.

For Jarrow lad Finnigan, signing for Shields was a return to his South Tyneside roots, attracted by King's patter and the ambition of the club.

Finnigan's arrival strengthened a forward line which already had David Foley from the previous season and Gavin Cogdon, who had joined in June from Spennymoor. Legendary among Moors fans, having played a key role as they dominated the Northern League, scored in the 2013 FA Vase final and gained promotion up into the Evo-Stik Premier, Cogdon's arrival was another coup, not only illustrating their increased financial muscle but also the fresh pulling power of the hungry, fiercely ambitious club.

Those four signings were to prove highly influential players over the course of the season. Experienced, professional and still with a desire to learn despite having achieved so much in their careers, they were to become bedrocks of the side that was to go on to greatness, joining other top performers like Arca, Foley and Phillips.

They weren't the only signings that summer, though. King, like a kid in a sweet shop with a year's worth of pocket money, was determined to revamp his squad. In came the likes of David Palmer from Seaham, Matthew Wade and Dillon Morse from Blyth Spartans, ex-Blackburn Rovers youngster David Carson, Louis Storey from Team Northumbria and Dunston UTS goalkeeper Liam Connell, widely regarded as the best shot-stopper in the Northern League. Another keeper, Chris Elliott, was signed after international clearance was received from the Swedish FA, making three goalkeepers at the club with Joss Carmichael also in the frame.

With the likes of Danny Carson, Michael Turner, Ben Riding, Stephen Ramsey, Barrie Smith and Warren Byrne all still at the club from the promotion season, it meant there were plenty of options and no little ability at the new management team's disposal.

Picton, having been at the club throughout the summer, knew what he was coming into but for Fenton, it was more of a blank canvas. While he knew the style of some of the charges now at his disposal, finding out about their mentality was just as important.

"We had to sort out characters and the first training session I came to I asked if I could speak to each of them individually, just have three, four, five minutes to speak to them and see what I thought, make opinions on them in a real brief period of time.

"We are very similar also in terms of the type of people we like to work with. After the first session I'd already identified people, without any input from Lee, and his opinions were exactly the same on those characters. At any club you go in, you work through who the people you see who are going to benefit the football club, take it forward, and the people who are going to be surplus."

Those who were considered surplus on almost a snap judgement, however, were given a chance to prove themselves. There were no signings made by the new regime until every player had been assessed, both on the pitch and off it, in training and in the changing room.

It was inevitable that some would fall by the wayside. Before long, Turner, the hero just a few months earlier, left to join Morpeth Town. Riding also departed the club, seeking more regular first-team football while Byrne went on loan to Seaham, with Palmer and Elliott also heading for the exit door.

The biggest casualties, however, were the Carson brothers. The talented family were well known in South Tyneside and when the older of the two, Danny, had swapped Jarrow Roofing for Shields, it had caused quite the stir, with Roofing boss Richie McLoughlin hitting out at the Mariners.

"Since day one of this season, we've had to fend off approaches for our players from South Shields," McLoughlin said. "With the financial backing Shields have, can they not get their own players in or do they need me to scout for them first, then for them to take players directly from us?

"We're in a position where holidays and vastly-inflated wages are being thrown at players.

"Is there a strategy in place for Shields to rise at our expense?"

The younger Carson, David, had also enjoyed a spell at at Roofing, before moving to Ashington and eventually making the step up to Blackburn after a successful trial. When his time at Ewood Park came to a close, King earmarked him as one of his key targets.

Whatever bond David had enjoyed with King, however, he didn't seem to enjoy similar relations with the new regime. The defeat to North Shields, a seminal moment in the season, was the beginning of the end for the younger Carson. Rumours abounded of a bust-up behind the scenes and before November was out, Shields had announced his departure from the club, and in a break from the often tired, PR guff, released a statement stating that the "working relationship between management and the player had deteriorated".

David's exit saw many predict Danny would soon follow, and they weren't wrong. He was on his way in the first week of December, leaving a defensive gap at the club that the management moved quickly to plug with the signing of Alex Nicholson from Blyth Spartans, who could match Carson's versatility with the ability to play on either full-back flank or in midfield. Having also captured Anthony Callaghan, an attacking left-back, suddenly the South Shields squad under the joint managers was taking shape.

While Thompson had been ruthless in his decision-making, Picton and Fenton had also shown they knew exactly wanted from the people working for them.

"I don't care what anybody says, if we'd kept the same personnel that we inherited as a management team, if we'd kept them for the rest of the season, we wouldn't have a single trophy in that cabinet come the end of the season," Picton insists.

"It was a mentality thing more than anything else, and a professionalism thing. They wouldn't be here at the club in the first place if they couldn't play.

"There were some really good signings in the summer, 100%, but there was such a wide range in the spectrum of mentality that it was the first thing we needed to address. To be fair, the approach we took was that we gave everybody a chance until they proved otherwise. We were really clear in the direction and the standards that we were looking for and we gave each and every player the opportunity to come through and follow us. Then, as we got to various stages, certain players weren't able to come along on the journey, but everybody got their chance."

Fenton and Picton's first game in charge together came 24 hours after their appointment when they hosted Washington at Mariners Park. There was no time to prepare players or work on the training ground, but one immediate tactical move they implemented was reverting to a flat back four. Against Whitley Bay, in King's last game in charge, Shields had begun the match with the 3-5-2 system the manager had begun to favour, only for Adam Shanks to twice exploit huge gaps in the home defence to put the away side 2-1 up at half-time.

There were further chances after the break for a pacy Bay team to increase their lead and it was only once the Mariners switched to a more conventional 4-4-2 formation, with the introduction of Briggs, Phillips and Finnigan from the bench, that they rescued the game.

It had become evident that there was a conflict in terms of tactics between King and his assistant Picton. The manager, in the second game of the season, had ripped up the plans his coach had worked studiously on throughout the summer with Shields trailing to Consett, a move which helped rescue a point but did little to create a sense of unity and clarity in the camp for both players and management.

"I let Lee look after everything in pre-season and he just wanted total football, everything played out from the back," admitted King. "I want football but there were times when you just couldn't play that way.

"One such game was the Consett game, we were 3-0 down at half-time and I hadn't touched anything. Lee had put a lot of hard work in during pre-season but it got to a point where I just thought 'fuck this'. I thought 'I've brought in all of these players and I could be losing my job here', so I changed it and went 3-5-2 and we came back and drew 3-3."

When Picton went on holiday, King used the 3-5-2 system at Chester-le-Street and then the long trip to Penrith, with success, as 6-0 and 2-0 victories finally got their season up and running. Former Gateshead captain and stalwart defender Ben Clark had been added to the squad, Arca was operating as a left wing-back and up front, Shaw was banging in the goals, but against Bay the unit was less cohesive and it needed three goals and a change of formation in the last 20 minutes to turn the game around.

If King and Picton were perhaps not singing from the same hymn sheet, there was never going to be any such issue between the new management team. Working hand in glove for seven years at Monkseaton, Picton and Fenton had developed a successful style of coaching and managing that had led the Academy to six national finals, numerous county titles and helped produce a number of players who went on to forge careers in the US and elsewhere.

While they were head coach and assistant coach at Monkseaton, it was in essence a partnership and one which continued to flourish at Shields.

While both men have different character traits and at times appear chalk and cheese, their football philosophy is completely in tandem.

"We've got very similar beliefs," says Fenton. "I enjoyed working with Lee for seven years and had learned a lot in that period. We have similar principles so it was never going to be a case that we couldn't make it work."

If there had been any uncertainty about how South Shields were going to play previously, that was quickly dispelled by the new management. With King watching on from the sidelines, Washington were beaten 3-1 to send the Mariners top of the table but five of the starting line-up that night would not be at the club by the turn of the year, including Clark who limped off with a groin injury midway through the first half and soon retired to focus on coaching.

His absence was compounded when, a couple of games later, Storey suffered a broken leg in the 4-1 win at West Auckland as South Shields' central defensive options suddenly looked limited, but necessity is often the mother of invention and whether it was through luck, judgement or happenstance, a partnership was borne in the middle of the backline which was to be the bedrock for the rest of the season and beyond.

Shaw had already shown he had lost none of his attacking guile, certainly at a level way below the standard he was used to scoring at, but when Picton approached him about moving back into defence as a makeshift centre half, he jumped at the chance.

"It was something I'd mentioned to Lee and Jon in the summer," he said. "It was something I wanted to do at some point but when I went back there I didn't think it would be long-term, I thought it would be a few games and they would bring someone in."

It was a move initially viewed with some scepticism, especially given further injuries to Mariners strikers Cogdon and Foley, but the decision to play one of the league's most feared forwards as a central defender proved to be inspired.

It was not that Shaw hadn't had experience of playing there before. His latter days at Gateshead had seen him operate in a similar role and it was one he quickly looked at home in, alongside Morse, who grabbed his opportunity with both hands after a frustrating time on the sidelines. The duo kept clean sheets against Esh Winning and Jarrow Roofing as a partnership was born.

"It gave me a new lease of life," added Shaw. "It reinvigorated me.

"I've always talked to players in games and I like being able to organise."

The puzzle was gradually being pieced together though there was no sign of the other title challengers giving up without a fight. Bonfire Night proved to be the dampest of squibs for the Mariners as their 21-game unbeaten run was extinguished by North Shields in front of an incredible crowd of 2,651 who braved the wind, rain and hailstones to pack into the ground to watch the league's top two sides go head to head.

Kevin Hughes' late winner, after Arca had missed a first-half penalty, meant the visitors could return through the Tyne Tunnel with all three points, handing their former boss Fenton his first defeat since he quit the club. More importantly, it created an eight-point gap between the two teams which left South Shields forever having to play catch-up to their rivals.

The other outcome of that result was a wake-up call to both players and management that they needed to step up their levels even further. While they hadn't deserved to get beaten and the margins had been close, the management team felt they learned a lot about the character and mentality of their players that day, particularly in the last 10 minutes when, a goal down, the game petered out.

It needed a response and they got one. The nine remaining games in 2016 were all won as Shields ended the calendar year five points behind league leaders North Shields and still in all the cups, which were quickly to become their focus. Eight of the first eleven games of 2017 were in the knockout tournaments as progress in others competitions took precedence over the Northern League bid.

It was to be a stunning run of games, no more so than the FA Vase clash with an old rival.

PHOTOGRAPHS

Barrie Smith in action at Peterlee against Ryton in 2015. Only he and Stephen Ramsey survived from that era to the FA Vase win.

South Shields in action at Peterlee in 2015. In the background, you can see members of the committee who kept the club going

Julio Arca meets his new team-mates after signing for the Mariners.

Arca's debut against Stokesley

Long-serving committee man Dick Bailey is honoured for his service to the club over decades

FROM EDEN TO PARADISE

Warren Byrne scores his screamer against Tow Law. It went viral on the social media and won national and international awards.

Shields players celebrate with Byrne after his stunning goal at Tow Law.

Leepaul Scroggins swigs on a bottle of bubbly after South Shields won the Division Two title at Crook Town.

Fans, players and committee celebrate the Division Two title at Crook.

Barrie Smith _ Co celebrate after being presented with the Division Two trophy at Mariners Park.

Jon King and Gary Crutwell with the Division Two trophy

Jon King and his management team with the Division Two trophy.

Work begins at Mariners Park on the floodlit 3G pitch.

FROM EDEN TO PARADISE

Gary Crutwell hard at work on the Mariners Park pitch. He helped transform it into one of the best surfaces in non-league football.

A fan tries on a Geoff Thompson mask

Lights out! Darkness - and controversy - descends at Mariners Park in the FA Vase tie against Morpeth after a floodlight failure.

Gavin Cogdon celebrates scoring in the rearranged Vase tie against Morpeth

ROSS GREGORY

Robert Briggs_ late winner in the FA Vase v Runcorn Linnetts.

Kit man George McLaughlin gets a hand from Andrew Stephenson.

Shields produced a stellar first-half performance against Newport Pagnall in the FA Vase in front of 3,000 fans

David Foley's injury-time winner at Coleshill in the first leg of the Vase semi-final.

FROM EDEN TO PARADISE

Shields players celebrate at Coleshill

Fans jammed into Mariners Park for the second leg of the Vase semi-final.

Louis Storey's last-gasp winner at Newcastle Benfield was crucial in the 2016-17 title race.

Julio Arca and Gavin Cogdon both scored in the league win over Sunderland RCA, a game which many saw as the turning point in the 2016-17 title chase.

ROSS GREGORY

Robert Briggs and Jon Shaw celebrate beating North Shields 1-0 to secure an unofficial world record 31st consecutive win.

The dressing room at Ashington after Shields sealed the Division One title.

Celebrating in the sun after being presented with the Division One trophy.

Jon Shaw lifts the Durham Challenge Cup at Hartlepool

FROM EDEN TO PARADISE

The committee from the Peterlee days pictured at the FA Vase Final press day

Lee Picton and Graham Fenton stride out at Wembley for the FA Vase final.

Carl Finnigan celebrates becoming the first South Shields player to score at Wembley.

Shields management team Lee Picton and Graham Fenton (middle) celebrate just after the final whistle with kitman George McLaughlin

ROSS GREGORY

South Shields lift the FA Vase after beating Cleethorpes at Wembley

Julio Arca gets his hands on the trophy.

The open top bus tour through South Shields saw a turn out of thousands of people.

Chairman Geoff Thompson addresses the Bents Park crowd after the bus parade.

FROM EDEN TO PARADISE

A civic reception for the quadruple-winning squad

The four trophies won in the historic, unprecedented 2016-17 season. Will it ever be matched?

A well-deserved testimonial for Stephen Ramsey, after 10 years with the club through thick and thin. Pictured with Geoff Thompson and secretary Phil Reay.

The BBC prepare to provide online coverage of South Shields FA Cup tie against Bridlington Town.

ROSS GREGORY

Ex-Newcastle midfielder and South Africa international Matty Patttison celebrates with Robert Briggs after scoring in the FA Cup.

CHAPTER EIGHT

JANUARY 7, 2017. 4.39PM…

Morpeth Town forward Liam Henderson picks the ball up on the edge of the South Shields box.

He takes a touch, lifts his head. Jon Shaw and Craig Baxter are slow to close him down. Henderson, at Watford as a youngster, needs no second invitation to show the class that saw him play in the Football League for the Hornets. His right-foot effort arcs up and over Liam Connell in the South Shields goal, bouncing over the line off the crossbar.

It's a stunning goal, Morpeth's fourth of the afternoon at Mariners Park. Henderson briefly stands still, one arm aloft, before starting to wheel towards the corner flag as the Highwaymen players rush to congratulate him but before they reach the striker the pitch is submerged in darkness.

It would later be called a "catastrophic failure" of the floodlights. It would later see acrimonious and bitter accusations of foul play levelled at South Shields, particularly vice-chairman Gary Crutwell. It would later be seen as the moment the Mariners' name was written on the FA Vase.

Just over four seconds had passed between the ball nestling in the back of the net and the floodlights going out. Just over four months later, as Shields boarded the bus to Wembley, the controversy, claims and anger were still raging.

The FA Vase tie was, undoubtedly, the game of the fourth round, pitting together the holders against the favourites to dethrone them.

Morpeth, under the stewardship of joint-managers Nick Gray and Dave Malone, had sensationally lifted the Vase at Wembley eight months earlier, producing a stunning performance to beat former Football League side Hereford 4-1.

Hereford had headed into the game as huge favourites, looking for their fourth trophy of the season. Sound familiar, Shields fans? But despite taking the lead after just 75 seconds, they were no match for the Northumbrians as Morpeth came storming back to win the Vase, the seventh time in eight seasons a Northern League side had lifted the trophy.

Of those teams, only Whitley Bay had successfully defended the trophy, but Morpeth were determined to keep hold of the Vase for another 12 months. Gray and Malone had recruited strongly in the summer, bringing in the likes of Henderson from Spennymoor Town, ex-Newcastle United youngster Mark Doninger and three-times Vase winner Paul Robinson, dubbed the 'Hillheads Maradona' during his time at Whitley Bay.

Morpeth's squad was arguably stronger and better than the previous season as Gray and Malone, backed by their hugely passionate and ambitious chairman Ken Beattie, targeted not only a repeat of their Wembley heroics but also the league title, which evaded them as they ran out of steam after playing catch up to a backlog of games.

The turn of the year saw Morpeth somewhat off the pace again in the Division One title race. Like South Shields, they'd had a slow start, winning just four of their opening eight league games as North Shields continued to streak ahead at the top of the table.

The Highwaymen, however, had already showed their undoubted class in the cup competitions. A sensational FA Cup run had seen them win four qualifying round games, including producing a phenomenal performance to beat neighbours Blyth Spartans 4-2 at Croft Park. It was a result which gave famed cup giantkillers Blyth a taste of their own medicine. Spartans sprang to prominence in 1978 with a historic run to the fifth round where they lost a replay against Wrexham and in recent years, had made the third round in 2008, losing to Premier League opposition Blackburn Rovers and then again in 2014, when as an Evo-Stik Premier side they led Championship outfit Birmingham City 2-0 before running out of gas and losing 3-2.

Just two years later, they were dumped out of the same competition they had tasted so much success in, on a receiving end of their own as Morpeth put them to the sword, having seen off Colwyn Bay in another big upset the round previous. Henderson justified his signing with the clincher in a 4-2 win after the Highwaymen had initially stormed into a 3-0 lead before Spartans mounted a comeback.

Morpeth were to eventually bow out of the competition at National League side Altrincham in the next round, unable to produce a third upset in a row but a month later they got their Vase defence under way with a comfortable 4-0 win at Hallam.

IF THE SHIELDS tie was to hit the headlines, it was nothing compared to the win Morpeth enjoyed - and endured - in the game that set up the fourth round tie.

A 3-2 victory at fellow Northern League side Newton Aycliffe was edgy in more ways than one as footage emerged of Aycliffe players storming the visiting dressing room after the game, threatening the Town players in ugly scenes that brought shame on the league. The video footage went viral and and generated unsavoury headlines not just in the North East, but on a national scale. Morpeth's players and staff were cleared of any wrongdoing, but the incident cost Aycliffe manager Peter Dixon his job as the Durham-based club sacked him a couple of days later and also released a number of players caught up in the clashes.

If the FA felt that was the Vase's controversy over for the season, events on January 7, sadly, proved otherwise.

Everything was set up for a crackerjack of a fixture. Bookmakers had installed Shields as favourites to win the Vase, with Morpeth second in the betting. It stood to reason that whoever came through this tie as victors would have a very strong chance of getting to Wembley and lifting the trophy.

Morpeth were in fine form coming into the game, having scored 14 goals in their previous two games, an 8-1 hammering of Chester-le-Street and a 6-3 triumph over Bishop Auckland. And while neither side sat atop of the Division One table - Morpeth were 14 points adrift of leaders North Shields with four games in hand and nine points behind second-placed South Shields having played three games fewer - most non-league aficionados recognised these two teams as the best in the Northern League.

The Mariners, too, were in good form, having won 10 games on the trot in all competitions and 19 of their last 20 matches, which included a stunning 4-0 win at Morpeth in the league. For many, this game was too close to call.

As ever, Picton and Fenton had set their team up with a game-plan in mind, strict instructions of how to play to beat their opponents, and for the first 10 minutes everything appeared to be going to plan.

Foley opened the scoring in the seventh minute with a goal which showcased why Shields were such a threat. While they were synonymous with playing good football, a patient build-up and moving the ball through the thirds, they also had the ability to be more direct, getting the ball over the full-backs' heads for the pace of Cogdon and Foley, who loved to pull into wide areas. Finnigan's presence also added an aerial threat to the Mariners' frontline, and it was a combination of these two tactics that brought about the opener.

Foley had been instructed to drift out right to try and get in behind Morpeth left-back Michael Turner, and when Connell launched a long ball towards Finnigan's head, the trap was set. Finnigan duly won the flick-on, and Foley caught Turner napping to steal in beyond him and slide the ball into the bottom corner.

At this point it was all South Shields. Foley and Finnigan went close to a second but against the run of play, a rare Craig Baxter error gifted Shaun Taylor the chance to level for Morpeth and he made no mistake.

The momentum had swung. Afterwards, the Shields management

duo admitted it was as if their players had switched off but Morpeth, having been under the cosh for the first 20 minutes, now looked like a side befitting of being the holders of the competition.

The excellent Ben Sayers broke through the middle of the pitch on a counter-attack, and as Arca chased him down, he was harshly adjudged to have clipped his heels. A foul was given and a yellow card issued to the Argentine star. It was an incident which would have repercussions not long after.

The game was now becoming fractious. The tension in the air was palpable as a crowd in excess of 1,500 bayed for every decision and tackles became full-blooded. Nicholson was cynically fouled by Sayers as he broke away just before the interval, the Morpeth man rightly booked, and Arca stood over the free-kick with the chance to swing over a cross that could help send the home side in at the interval ahead.

His set-piece was poor, headed away at the front post but worse was to come for the Shields captain. As he contested the loose ball on the touchline with Liam Henderson, the two players went to ground amid a tangle of legs, a minor scuffle and an eyeball-to-eyeball confrontation on the ground.

"Just a bit of argy-bargy," commented one fan, no pun intended.

Morpeth thought otherwise and their experienced schemer Keith Graydon made a beeline for referee Aaron Bannister to protest his case against Arca and after consultation with his assistant, the match official flashed a second yellow card was shown to the midfielder and he was off.

"Did you think it was a sending off?" asked Fenton some time later.

I did. While it may not have been the worst crime committed on a football pitch, having been booked just minutes earlier, Arca had given the referee a decision to make.

"I disagree," said Fenton. "The sending off turned everything their way."

Regardless of the rights and wrongs, Shields now had a mountain to climb. Faced with the prospect of playing the entire second half with 10 men, Fenton and Picton had a big teamtalk to give. The game was far from lost at this stage, but it would need a huge 45 minutes from the home side to keep out the Vase holders.

Intriguingly, when the Mariners came out for the second period, there had been a tactical switch, but not the way many may have predicted. Arca's absence from the centre of midfield hadn't prompted Picton and Fenton to sacrifice a forward to strengthen the centre of the park. Rather, they sacrificed a defender, going three at the back in a bid to stay on the front foot.

Baxter was switched from right back to become the left-sided central defender alongside Morse and Shaw, with Nicholson moving from his left-back role to a position on the right side of the midfield diamond, with Briggs in the centre alongside Richardson - who had come on in the first half for the injured Andrew Stephenson - and Wayne Phillips on the left, leaving the strikeforce of Finnigan and Foley intact, although the former was expected to drop deeper.

It was a bold move and it appeared to be the right one when, within seven minutes of the restart, Shields stormed into the lead again. Morse sent a looping header goalwards after a corner hadn't been fully cleared by the Morpeth defence, only for Graydon to acrobatically clear off the line. The ball fell to Shaw, who returned it into the penalty area where Richardson ghosted in to slip the ball past Dryden in the Morpeth goal.

Cue more bedlam in the ground as the crowd erupted. Could Shields really do this?

Perhaps now was the time to switch system again, revert to a flat back four and pack the midfield? Not so for the Shields management duo, confident in their tactics.

Morpeth came again, pressing for a leveller. Henderson rifled inches wide but the equaliser was coming and after another set-piece was only half cleared, Turner rifled home low into the corner to draw the sides level again.

Still Shields refused to lie down. A breakaway led to Foley's shot from distance being saved before another contentious decision when Finnigan claimed a penalty after a tangle of legs in the box, though the striker appeared to make the most of the incident.

Morpeth were the bigger goal threat, however, with South Shields' right-hand side a real weakness. Long diagonal balls from

Graydon out to Taylor found him isolating Morse, with Nicholson unable to offer protection, and Turner's overlapping runs were proving a real menace.

Shields were scrambling, with last-ditch headers, challenges and bodies thrown on the line to keep their goal intact but the mental side was as much of a problem as the physical element. A short corner for Morpeth saw Shields switch off and with only one man going out to close down, Taylor was left in acres to rasp a shot at goal. It struck a forest of legs and rebounded to the edge of the box where Graydon was lurking, unfortunately for the Mariners to the one man they didn't want the ball to fall to. He stepped forward onto the rolling ball and powered it with such controlled force that it sped past Connell and hit the back of the net before the goalkeeper had barely time to react.

It was a stunning strike, worthy of winning any game, never mind one as pulsating and tension-filled as this one, and showcased the ability of the Irishman which had earned him the reputation as one of the best non-league midfielders in the region.

With almost half an hour to go, though, it was never going to be the final word of a cup tie that had everything - including a phantom red card. Shields had responded to the setback by introducing Cogdon from the bench for his first outing after injury and his impact was immediate, spinning Turner and racing to the edge of the box before being brought down by the Morpeth left-back. Referee Bannister was quickly on the scene, brandishing a yellow card and then a red to Turner.

Mariners Park erupted again. Here was their big chance to get back into the game, with the teams now levelled up at 10 men apiece. Morpeth and Turner, in particular, were apoplectic and it took almost two minutes for the situation to be resolved amid much confusion and conjecture before Bannister figured out he'd not previously booked Turner and he was allowed to remain on the pitch.

By this time, the referee had lost control, some may say lost the plot. Cries of "you don't know what you're doing" rang out around the game and it was hard to disagree with the chants. Morpeth substitute Steven Anderson went in high and late on Baxter as the game threatened to boil over and from the resultant free-kick,

Richardson was shoved in the back just inside the penalty area, only for Bannister, who by now was surely wishing the game would come to a premature end, to wave away the penalty claims as Richardson lay on the ground.

If Finnigan's appeal had been debatable, this looked a nailed-on penalty and only added to the sense of outrage and injustice for the Mariners fans and players.

Shields were scrapping for their lives and Briggs came within a stud length of sliding in a tempting Cogdon cross, but Morpeth were always the bigger goal threat as they began to pick further holes in a tiring defence. Taylor was the key man, patrolling the inside left channel of the visitors' attack, teeing up first Paul Robinson for an effort which arced just off target before, with nine minutes remaining, helping set up what turned out to be the game's final act.

Taylor, held up by Morse, laid the ball off to Turner, advancing once again from left-back. His pass inside eventually dropped to Henderson who sent a stunning, dipping, curling effort in off the crossbar and began to wheel away in celebration, knowing that with such little time left, a 4-2 lead and a man advantage, it was almost game over.

What happened from that moment on became the subject of accusations, counter-claims, threats of legal action and an FA investigation.

With the ball still not entirely motionless after ricocheting over the line, Mariners Park was suddenly plunged into darkness as the floodlights went out. At first it seemed comical, but as time elapsed with no sign of them coming back on, it became increasingly obvious that the game wouldn't be finished.

Behind the scenes, Crutwell - whose role as vice-chairman included managing the site - tried manfully to fix the generator. It wasn't the first time this had happened at Mariners Park and Crutwell was hoping to call upon his experience of fixing the problem, having managed successfully twice the previous season.

Morpeth chairman Ken Beattie was taking a keen interest and had called on the services of a couple of fans who were electrical engineers to help, but despite the efforts of all involved the game was ultimately abandoned and the outcome left in the hands of the FA.

Conspiracy theorists pointed to the fact that the lights in the clubhouse were still on, as were those on the newly-installed 4G pitch behind the bottom goal. The later explanation that these were run off a different power supply failed to stop the rumours.

By the end of the Saturday evening, the abandonment was trending all over Twitter. One wag had mocked up a picture of Arca running away with a fuse under his arm and every Northern League player or fan appeared to have an opinion on what had happened or what should be the outcome.

Understandably, Morpeth were raging. Joint-manager Dave Malone and Graydon left no one under any illusions as to how the club felt in their after-match interviews and what they thought the FA should decide.

"I think the FA should use common sense and give us the tie," Graydon told Highwaymen TV. "If this had been the other way around, and it goes to the FA, I'm sure Morpeth Town would have done the right thing and awarded South Shields the result if they were ahead.

"It's in the hands of the FA but it's really frustrating. I think common sense should prevail. If it's 60 minutes in, it's a different story but with nine minutes to go in the game, a two-goal lead, them down to 10 men, realistically they should give us the tie."

Malone echoed those thoughts, and warned of a potential impact further down the line if the FA ordered the tie must be played again. His inference that there may have been some skullduggery going on, however, was what angered South Shields FC most.

"If that game doesn't stand, it leaves a precedent for all other teams who are getting beaten up and down the country," he said. "Who knows if it was an accident, we can't tell, but it's a mighty coincidence that when the fourth goal goes in, the lights go off.

"Like I say, I'm not saying it's been done deliberately, but with nine minutes to go in a game, if you're not awarded that game with two goals up and the other team has 10 men, then it could happen all over the country."

The idea that there had been any deliberate act of sabotage privately infuriated South Shields, but they opted to keep their own counsel. Over the next 48 hours, the FA asked the home club for a report into what had happened and sent their own inspector out to look at the generator, while arguments raged on over whether the Mariners should just concede the game while the FA Vase rulebook was consulted by almost everyone.

It was a decision the club, and Geoff Thompson, mulled over considerably but decided, ultimately, to leave in the hands of the game's governing body who 48 hours after the abandonment, stated there was "no fault of either club" and the tie must be replayed in accordance with competition rule 11 section C, which states: "When a first match has been postponed, or is abandoned before the completion of 90 minutes and neither club being at fault, it shall be played on the same ground on or before the following Saturday."

The game was rescheduled for the Wednesday, at Mariners Park, but if anyone thought that was the end of the matter, they were wrong.

Shields, by now keen to get their version of events out to the public, released a statement in which they hit back at "unfair criticism and scurrilous attacks on its integrity".

It read: "In the 81st minute of the tie, seconds after Morpeth took a 4-2 lead, there was a catastrophic failure of the diesel generator that provides power to the main floodlights. The generator is totally independent of all the other lighting within the ground and its local vicinity.

"Attempts were made for 45 minutes after the failure to restart the generator without success. Morpeth Town officials were present and indeed a suitably-qualified Morpeth supporter was also in attendance.

"Following consultation between the referee and the FA, at 5.30pm the match was declared abandoned.

"The club was required to submit a report by 9am today to the FA detailing the circumstances of the failure, which resulted in the club being exonerated from any fault on its part. Further, by 5pm today we were required to supply the FA with an independent report from a qualified Electrical Contractor together with photographic evidence of the present state of the generator.

"The FA, having found nothing untoward, have applied their

published rules, which requires the match to be replayed at Mariners Park at the earliest opportunity.

"The club historically has relied upon a power supply remote from the site. Our own dedicated supply was ordered and paid for in June 2016 and is scheduled to be energised before the end of January 2017. At that stage, all of the ground's electrical requirements will be provided by a mains feed directly under the control of the club, thus hopefully alleviating any future problems."

Less than 24 hours later, Morpeth had responded themselves with a statement of their own. I'd spoken to Ken Beattie that day when he claimed had the shoe been on the other foot, he would have conceded the game and he called on Geoff Thompson to do so himself, but with the tie now set to be replayed, he wanted his own version of events made public, disputing many of the claims made by the Mariners.

It read: "Let us state at this stage that Morpeth Town have enormous respect for all the good people behind the scenes at South Shields, and its wonderful supporters who back the club so amicably and help make it the huge success story it is.

"We feel, however it is very important to let everyone know what our versions of the facts are, not only to make it clear to all what happened, but to create a position where lessons can be learnt in order such incidents do not reoccur.

"South Shields have, up until now, relied upon a diesel driven engine which drives a generator, thereby creating electricity for the club.

"On Saturday the generator did not catastrophically fail, it was the engine driving the generator that was starved of diesel either by a break in the fuel lines or a blockage in the system. In the case of Saturday, any blockage or air lock would almost certainly have been in the area of the filters (borne out by historical data at South Shields). When the fuel failed to reach the compression area of the engine it came to a natural halt, the generator then stopped working and the lights went out. This was confirmed by the Morpeth electrical mechanical engineers who were present.

"To compound the problem of fuel starvation, the batteries had gone flat after multiple attempts to start the engine when under full load and still connected to the live system. It is normal practise when restarting a diesel engine to isolate the load and then start the generator in a stabilized condition. This situation was rectified by the engineers but by this time, the battery was too flat to operate with no back-up batteries.

"It is unfortunate that procedures at South Shields had not been followed as in a number of previous instances, such as against Willington FC (when) in near identical circumstances, they managed to diagnose and fix the problem by bleeding the system within a 40 minutes timeframe."

The finger had been firmly pointed at Crutwell for how he'd attempted to fix the generator, the inference being he hadn't followed the same procedures as in the past. Shields were livid. How did Morpeth know whether the circumstances were 'identical' to when the lights had gone out against Willington? Who were they to question the procedure and efforts, when the FA had ruled all was above board?

This time, they didn't respond, instead focusing their attention on ensuring the replayed game went ahead. The generator and lights were in such a bad way, however, that they couldn't be fixed in time for the new date so on the day of the game, the tie was switched to Morpeth's Craik Park, a beautiful ground set just outside the town.

Advantage Morpeth, surely. Picton and Fenton, however, were determined to take advantage of their second chance.

The one trick they had up their sleeve was Cogdon. His cameo in the abandoned game had been just 16 minutes long but he'd shown enough sharpness to persuade the managers that they should gamble on his fitness and hand him just his second start after two months out with a groin injury. Up against a big, physical defence, the plan was to load the top end of the pitch with as much pace as possible. It was an inspired move, with the Little and Little partnership of Cogdon and Foley terrorising the Morpeth back four in a sensational showing by Shields.

It may have been a different story entirely had Taylor, a real thorn in Shields' side in the original game, put away a glorious chance inside the first few minutes. The winger was left with a gaping goal but his left-foot effort skewed way off target.

Cogdon quickly showed him how it was done. Nine minutes were on the clock when Foley danced down the left wing and his low cross found his strike partner with his back to goal. The defending wasn't great, allowing him time and space, but the deft turn and venomous left-footed finish was the mark of a class act.

They may only have had a few hours to change their arrangements after the tie was switched to Morpeth, but the noise inside Craik Park when that goal went in showed how huge numbers of Sand Dancers had made the journey to Northumberland. They had barely settled down when they were cheering again as Richardson's through ball split the defence open and Foley got in behind Turner again to coolly roll home a second goal.

Within seconds of the restart, Morpeth were handed a golden opportunity to get back in the game. A rare error from Jon Shaw saw him bring down Henderson and the Highwayman had a penalty. Taylor stepped up, keen to atone for that early miss, but he only compounded his miserable start to the game by lifting his spot-kick way over the crossbar.

It had been an opening 13 minutes as pulsating as the original tie and just like the first game, there was controversy to come on the stroke of half-time. A Morpeth attack saw the ball land at the feet of Chris Reid on the left edge of the box and as he shaped to shoot, Baxter flung himself in the way of the ball. Reid's shot was on target but clearly hit the Shields defender's hand, prompting vociferous appeals for another penalty both on and off the pitch.

They were waved away and as Morpeth protested, Shields broke through Cogdon in the inside left channel. Advancing into the penalty area, he shimmied and slipped the ball through a defender's legs before nonchalantly lifting it over Dryden and into the net.

It was a wonderful goal, a moment of pure individual brilliance, and a dagger through Morpeth's hearts from which they could never recover. Having been 4-2 up and a man up with nine minutes left, they now found themselves 3-0 down at half-time and heading out of the competition they had been so desperate to retain.

It was hard not to feel some sympathy for Morpeth. The Highwaymen, ironically, felt that they had been robbed and their second-half performance was that of a team who knew their cup hopes were over. Shields threatened to grab a fourth goal on several occasions before Foley put the seal on an emphatic win with eight minutes remaining and there was still time for Graydon's frustrations to boil over with a wild challenge on Finnigan earning him a second yellow card of the night.

There were none of the usual pleasantries exchanged by members of each dugout at the final whistle. Instead, words were exchanged which left Fenton, for one, infuriated and snubbing interview requests afterwards.

Picton went before the camera but refused to talk about the previous few days, instead just focusing on the performance of his players that night. Morpeth boss Nick Gray spoke to his club's TV channel and while gutted and admitting there was a sense of injustice, wished Shields good luck.

It had been an emotional few days; at times bitter; often accusatory; always controversial. For many people, the incident left a nasty taste in the mouth which is still unpleasant on the palette even now. Relationships between the clubs and individuals, often fraught after recent situations, were damaged, but a hope remained that a line could be drawn in the sand.

Sadly, that wasn't the case and there was one final twist to come in 'Floodlightgate'. Two days before the Vase final, a statement from Beattie appeared on a prominent non-league forum, containing further allegations over what happened four months previous and what had gone on in the interim period, with several South Shields individuals mentioned.

It was enough for Shields to discuss whether to take legal action or not. The forum moderators were contacted and within 24 hours the post, and all the replies to it, had been removed.

By now for the Mariners, it was water under the bridge. They had a Wembley final to concentrate on and if the timing of the release was designed to upset their preparations, it didn't have the desired effect. There was some discussion over the content on the team coach on the way to London, but it was soon laughed off and forgotten about. There was a game to win and distractions weren't needed.

Looking back at the whole situation with hindsight, there are still a lot of mixed feelings for those caught up in the eye of the storm.

"I've always said that I'd be the same," said Picton on Morpeth's disappointment. "Literally ten seconds after the lights went out here I went and apologised to Nicky Gray and Kenny Beattie, who was already on the pitch at this point. I thought it was the right thing to do at the time.

"I used to play for Kenny's club myself and I always try, whenever I can, to empathise with other people. If the tables were turned I'd have been very very disappointed myself. But it's one of those things, it happened and there's nothing we could do about it. We followed the rules that were set down to us and we went on to get to the final.

"Was it the perfect scenario? Definitely not. But I still think we got there by merit."

What pleased the management most, however, was the attitude and application of their players in the period between the two fixtures. There was no Twitter banter, no loss of focus, just a steely determination to put things right and make the most of the second chance.

"From our perspective, and we communicated this to the players straight away, we just had to get on with things," Picton added. "It was almost nothing to do with us, it was an FA decision. We were given another opportunity and we told the players not get embroiled in any of that rubbish, just to be professional and get on with your job.

"One of the rules I try to live by and work by is that you try and control what you can control. I couldn't control what everybody else's reaction was to the situation - I could only control moving forwards what we could do as a side and that was my only focus. I didn't see any point whatsoever in wasting any energy.

"I'm not on social media but I see it as a complete waste of energy to try and argue the point. I always prefer to speak to people personally but in terms of preparing the team, we were told what the situation was and what we had to do, and we prepare the team as best we can and I think that showed in the following game, and the games subsequent.

"But I don't mind admitting that there was part of me that,

between the two games, thought I was frustrated because I knew what would be coming, I knew what certain people would think. Part of me thought 'do I really want to win it that way?'. But then there is also a large part of me who realised it wasn't anyone's fault."

Stuart Dick was Morpeth's media manager at the time. He feels the situation could have been handled better from all parties but that with emotions running high, there was always going to be some fall-out. Some you win, some you lose and Morpeth had benefited from an FA rule the season before on their way to Wembley. They'd been scheduled to play 1874 Northwich on a Saturday, only for their Craik Park pitch to be waterlogged.

Northwich had requested the game be rescheduled for the following Saturday, Morpeth had refused, the FA ruled it must be played on the Wednesday and Northwich promptly conceded the tie, saying they were unable to get a team out for the 400-mile round trip in midweek.

Dick said: "I think, personally, no matter what anyone says, that the tie was decided when those lights went out. It gave South Shields a second chance that they were never going to squander and as a club we probably felt a bit sorry for ourselves.

"We were taking on one of the best sides I've seen at the Northern League level, a team who'd already dismantled us in the league 4-0 earlier in the season. Over the last three seasons it has been a mammoth task for any side to beat South Shields, let alone twice in a week – especially in the circumstances.

"Both clubs could have handled it better, but South Shields did nothing wrong, Morpeth did nothing wrong. For me, it was case of the FA rule not being fit for purpose – and before people point out Morpeth won a game in walkover the year before, I also believe that rule was not fit for purpose."

The final word on it goes to Fenton.

"There's no two ways about it, we got away with one. But the accusations that have been thrown around since then have just been scandalous.

"To actually accuse someone of sabotage was ridiculous. Morpeth, as well as anyone, know floodlight failure can happen. It's happened at their ground on several occasions."

CHAPTER NINE

MARCH 18, 2017...

"Today we made history for the club, for ourselves and for the whole town. We are going to savour it tonight!"

The tears welled up in Julio Arca's eyes again. He quickly composed himself again, as questions continued to rain down on him. Local TV, radio, the Shields Gazette, club website all waiting patiently for the Argentinian to move on to them. Still decked out in his full kit, mud fresh on his knees and sweat glistening on his brow.

He finally finished and made his excuses. "I'm freezing, I need to get a shower now," he pleaded. "And a drink or two."

"Jooolio, Jooolio," went up the chant from the few remaining fans by the side of the pitch one last time. An hour earlier, almost three and a half thousand had sung exactly the same as he'd trooped from the pitch at half-time in the second leg of the FA Vase semi-final at Mariners Park. Seconds previously, his famous left peg had put Shields on the verge of Wembley.

What the 36-year-old had been doing on the edge of the Coleshill Town box at that exact moment remains a mystery. With the game delicately poised after a 2-1 win for Shields in the first leg, Arca's instructions had been to sit in front of the back four and prompt, protect.

"I could hear Jon Shaw saying, 'Jules, stay here' but I just decided to go."

Gavin Cogdon's cross couldn't have fallen to a better player. Twenty yards out, left foot. Coleshill goalkeeper Paul Hathaway barely saw the ball as it hurtled past him. I swear if there wasn't a net it would still be travelling now.

A screamer. And not the only scream.

Off went the little Argentine, voice shrieking in delight, drowned out only by the cheers of thousands of Sand Dancers both in ecstasy and relief.

After a tough first leg down in Warwickshire, where Coleshill gave the mighty Mariners a huge fright before Andrew Stephenson's injury-time winner, the visitors had shown no inclination of giving up without a fright.

They'd shown no sign of being overawed in that first period neither. A crowd of that magnitude, the majority crammed so tightly to the pitch that they can touch the players, can either inspire or intimidate. A month earlier, in front of a similar attendance, Newport Pagnell's players froze, blown away by the sheer scale of a crowd at Level 5 in the football pyramid and also a blistering start by South Shields in which they were 4-0 up inside 26 minutes.

That day, the attendance at Mariners Park topped all Conference crowds bar that at Wrexham, and was bigger than the majority of League Two games.

It finished 6-1, a demonstration of Shields' attacking potency. David Foley had set them on their way with a stunning, swerving opener before Wayne Phillips unleashed a rocket of his own. Dillon Morse powered in a header and Robert Briggs made it four with a phenomenal finish to a sweeping team move that made it three goal-of-the-season contenders in the first half.

Gavin Cogdon's brace after the break completed the rout and Shields were one step - or two games - from Wembley.

It's a splendidly curious part of English football that amateur, non-league footballers have just as much chance of playing at Wembley as the more talented, multi-millionaire stars gracing the upper echelons of the game, and Shields' squad this season was the epitome of that.

Arca's career had taken him from Argentinos Juniors to the Premier League, where he'd played more than 300 times, gracing every stadium from Old Trafford to Highbury. Yet never at Wembley. Contrast that with goalkeeper team-mate Liam Connell, who had never played higher than Northern League yet had played on the hallowed turf for Dunston UTS, winning the same competition back in 2012. Indeed half the Shields team had already appeared at the national stadium but the two players who had played at the highest level in their careers - Arca and Shaw - hadn't.

Now they were on the cusp of fulfilling that dream.

"It's the last tick on my football bucket list," said Shaw in the build-up to the semi-final second leg. "I've had a good career, I feel, and I've enjoyed it and had some great highs, but I've never been and played at Wembley."

The two men had done more than most in the first game against Coleshill to keep that dream alive. The first leg had been more a war of attrition rather than free-flowing football down in Warwickshire, Shields having to dig deep after a slow start which saw the home side threaten to bully and out-muscle the competition's favourites.

In the second half, when the pressure was piled on again, Shaw stood like a rock at the back, clearing and cajoling, organising his defence to cope with the barrage of long balls into the box. In front of him, Arca was immense. Scurrying and sliding, he showed the hunger and desire of someone desperate to get to the national stadium. There was composure and class too though. With the scores at 1-1 in the last 10 minutes, he received the ball under pressure just outside his own penalty area and drifted out towards the touchline. A Coleshill player advanced, sensing the opportunity to rob the Shields man of the ball in a dangerous area, potentially launching a match-winning situation.

For a second it looked like Arca had overrun the ball but it was all part of the ruse. The player was drawn in, tempted, and before he knew what had happened the ball had been pushed between his legs. Embarrassed by a bona fide star, at least he has something to tell the grandkids.

Arca scampered off, launching a counter-attack that relieved the pressure on his defence. Shields' very own safety valve dressed in claret and blue.

It was a brilliant last 20 minutes from the little master. If the game had been played on grass he'd have covered every blade of it. Instead, there wasn't a black pellet of the 4G surface that he didn't tread.

After the game, he sat on the concrete, back against one of the portacabins at Pack Meadow, phone in one hand and a cardboard plate of food by his side looking as far from a man who had captained Argentina to an Under-20 World Cup crown as you could imagine.

He had just been approached, by a Sunderland fan and now Coleshill committee man desperate for a word and a handshake, proud as punch that one of his biggest heroes had graced their modest ground.

It was a world away from those heady days. Now playing as an amateur, the professional game was long behind him but for a weekend, at least, it had been like old times. Shields had prepared properly for the semi-final, travelling down to the Midlands on Friday afternoon and staying over in a luxury spa hotel. It was one used by Graham Fenton during his Aston Villa days - "I think we stopped here before we played Inter Milan" - and it allowed the players to relax before the big day.

While they enjoyed a team meal on arrival, for the committee men who had travelled down it was straight to the hotel bar. Gary Crutwell and big pal Brian Lawson bickering like two old women, media man Daniel Prince drinking strawberry cider. I'd joined them for a couple of pints, which became a couple more, then a couple more after that. By this time, Picton and Fenton had also pulled up a chair having sent the players packing to their rooms.

I asked both if they missed playing. Picton, forced to quit through a back injury, was a yes. Coaching and managing gave him a buzz, but not like playing did.

Fenton, less so. "I don't miss being run ragged by kids, like it was in the last few days at Blyth!"

Fenton had finished his playing days at the famous non-league side, returning to his native North East after a career that had seen him play in spells at Aston Villa, Blackburn Rovers, Leicester City and St Mirren. Two League Cup winners medals, with Villa in 1994 and Leicester six years later (albeit he didn't appear in the final) were good reward for a solid pro. More domestic medals than Alan Shearer.

Not as many as John Regis, mind. The one-time Olympic sprinter was dining in the hotel's restaurant that same night, resplendent in a white shirt and looking as fit as he did when he won relay medals at Seoul in 1988 and Barcelona four years later.

Let's get him to record a message for Mariners TV, came the cry, until finally with enough Dutch courage inside them, Daniel and managing director Mike Orr approached the athlete, making sure he'd finished his meal first. A gent, Regis obliged, and came up with the most withering put-down later as he passed our group on his way through the bar. Brian Lawson, by this time 'well-served' as the saying goes, engaged in some banter with the Olympian.

"I bet I can run faster than you now," he jibed. Regis, taking one look at Brian's full figure, didn't miss a beat. "Looks like you can eat faster than me too."

Regis wasn't the only famous face stalking Shields that weekend. Darren Bent, once of Sunderland, turned up at Pack Meadow to watch the game. He didn't say who he was supporting but if it had been the Midlands team he'd have left disappointed by Stephenson's injury time winner.

The goal sent the hundreds of Mariners fans who had made the long journey down to Coleshill into raptures. Well almost all, anyhow. As the players trudged back into the Portacabins for a shower, one woman vented her spleen.

"That's the worst game I've seen them play. Bloody useless."

That's the price of success. With investment and progress comes greater standards and higher expectations. There was nothing to suggest she was a Jonny-come-lately to the club - she was certainly old enough to have been around in the Simonside Hall days - but if that was the worst she'd seen Shields play, having won the first leg of a national tournament's semi-final, then perhaps she hadn't watched many games.

It was a stutter, a minor bump in the road to Wembley, nothing like the roadblock that Morpeth had put in their way.

The players knew they hadn't been at their best, but it was their 23rd successive win. Twenty three! The coach trip home was livelier than the one down to Coleshill, beer on board after a quick stop at the local Tesco, but still not a raucous singalong session. The job was only half done, no time for celebrations yet.

They would come seven days later.

Arca's thunderbolt on the stroke of half-time settled the nerves. And there had been plenty. Sat in the main stand, you could hear the grumbles as Shields struggled to get the breakthrough, a product of tension from the faithful, some who had already pre-booked their travel, hotels and tickets for May 21.

"Get it forward!"

"Howay man, Wayne, get stuck in."

"Lump it up."

Shields would do anything but 'lump it up', sticking to the footballing principles espoused by Picton and Fenton, instead trying to 'play through the thirds'. Recycling of possession, building from the back, pop pop pop, pass pass pass.

There's an old cliche in football that the ball doesn't get tired, but players do and that's what happened to Coleshill after the break. Demoralised by the timing of Arca's strike, once Cogdon expertly added a second just after the hour mark - sitting the goalkeeper on his arse before deftly, nonchalantly lifting the ball over him - it was game over. Cogdon performed a handstand while kissing the turf, while behind him Hathaway was on his backside and the remaining Coleshill players were on their knees.

Carl Finnigan added a third before David Foley completed the rout in the last minute. Cue the pitch invasion at the final whistle, hundreds of fans ignoring the tannoy announcement to stay off the playing surface as kids and adults alike, resplendent in their replica shirts, made a sea of claret and blue.

Arca shed tears - of joy, he would later reveal - while Barrie Smith, on as a second-half substitute, was overcome with emotion, hugging his two sons Harvey and Riley on the pitch. For a journeyman Northern League player to be heading to Wembley, it was almost too much to comprehend.

"Days like this are what you dream of. Me and Julio, first time at Wembley, even though he's much more high-profile than I've ever been in my life.

"I've been with the club through all the hard times and to be here with the club now with the players and management we've got is amazing. And for the fans, they've been unbelievable, to get them to Wembley, as well as ourselves, it's hard to take in.

"Never in a million years did I think we'd be back here at Mariners Park, never mind playing in front of three and a half thousand unbelievable fans. The support is unreal. I'm over the moon for the whole club - fans, players, staff, the committee. You've got the likes of Bob Wray, Phil Reay, Gary Crutwell, the list can go on. They've been here through thick and thin."

Bob Wray had missed Julio's goal, too busy sorting money out in the office. He'd heard the roar, as they probably did two miles away on King Street. Phil Reay had been prowling pre-match. Now he was bear-hugging everyone and anyone out on the pitch.

Quiet and understated as ever, Gary was getting on with the job in hand. More than two hours later, with the celebrations still going on in the bar above him as players and fans mixed in together, he was walking around the ground picking up empty crisp packets, cans and other assorted rubbish with his litter-picker.

"I should have delegated this better," he grinned. "But I'll be here late enough celebrating – don't you worry."

Celebrate he did. As did many others. Cars were abandoned for the evening as the party raged on at the ground before spilling into town for a spot of clubbing. Smith was turned away from renowned nightspot Glitterball, on grounds of his alcohol consumption. It wasn't the first time he'd suffered that fate, with echoes of Southampton two months earlier still fresh in the mind. On that occasion, after a fifth round win over Team Solent, the team had stayed down south an extra night, bonding over beer with the hundreds of supporters who had travelled the length of the country to support them.

In years to come, that weekend may be seen as a turning point for the club. It's one thing building home crowds - and it's vital for a football club to have a loyal fanbase which will keep the coffers full - but those away followings are what sets you apart from the norm.

The North East is traditionally strong in this area. Both Newcastle United and Sunderland's away support is famed throughout the country. In times of economical and footballing hardship, fans on both sides of the Tyne-Wear divide have followed their club hundreds of miles across the country for very little reward.

Now it was South Shields' turn. Five hundred-plus supporters travelled by plane, train and automobile to cheer on their side against the students of Team Solent, a university outfit. It was a bigger away support than any other attendance in the Northern League that weekend.

Those who made the trip were treated to another piece of magic from the little master. With the dying embers of the game barely flickering, and Shields leading 4-2, Arca seized on a loose ball just inside the Solent half. One quick glance up was followed by a 45-yard chip which sailed over the stranded goalkeeper's head and into the net.

Talk about rolling back the years. Who needs David Beckham when Julio's in town?

A mini-pitch invasion ensued and a flare was let off and thrown onto the pitch. Both incidents were to later earn the club a slap on the wrists and a warning as to future conduct from the Football Association, a stark reminder that there are some parts of development which aren't always wanted.

It didn't mar the weekend, or the experience. Or the goal. Arca's 'worldie', captured on video, went viral, picked up by news associations across the country. Not on a Warren Byrne level mind, nor to the extent that was to happen a few weeks later with a save from Consett's Peter Jeffries against Shields, but still fair recognition for a fantastic piece of skill.

The game finished 5-2, not as comfortable a victory as the scoreline perhaps suggested. Team Solent had missed a penalty on the stroke of half-time with the game delicately poised at 1-1 and Shields had ridden their luck at times, before their class shone through.

No team will ever win a competition without a bit of good

fortune along the way. A lucky ricochet here, a floodlight failure there. But no team will ever win anything without talent, hard work and desire, either.

Nothing was left to chance. Preparation was key for Fenton and Picton, not only fine coaches but also perfectionists. Taking a walk around the outskirts of the Warwickshire hotel before the first Coleshill game, I'd asked Picton how the preparation had gone.

"We've done all we can," he said. "You've got to make sure you give players as few excuses as possible."

That even involved video analysis. The management duo are a firm believer in making sure nothing is left to chance, and for the Vase games they often commissioned videos of the opposition to scrutinise their style of play and set-pieces. Before Newport Pagnell arrived at Mariners Park, the Thursday session involved a 20-minute briefing upstairs going through 18 clips of free-kicks, corners and attacking situations before the players headed down to the training pitch to work on a number of routines themselves that Fenton had devised.

Twenty-six minutes into the tie, Dillon Morse rose unchallenged from a Wayne Phillips corner to head Shields 3-0 ahead. A similar situation had almost occurred against Team Solent, minus the vital finish, but it was further proof of the lengths and detail put into the preparation.

Picton had gone one further before facing Coleshill, watching random games in the Midland Premier League just to get an idea of the overall standard their opponents play at week in, week out.

There wasn't the need for such lengths in the early rounds of Shields' Vase run, as they'd faced familiar foes in Esh Winning and Marske United, fellow Northern League sides. There isn't much 'unknown' among Northern League teams. Many of the players have turned out for various clubs, managers work their way around the league and teams are watched regularly for a mix of scouting and snooping purposes. It's nosier than a Neighbourhood Watch convention.

Esh Winning, a struggling Division Two side, had been comprehensively dispatched in the second qualifying round, a 4-0 victory setting Shields on their way. That brought a first round tie against

Runcorn Linnets, flying high in the North West Premier Division and a tough test for the Mariners, one which they only overcame thanks to a dramatic stoppage-time winner from Briggs sealing a 2-1 win in a pulsating encounter.

And so on to Marske, Northern League champions in 2015 and runners-up 12 months later. It was the third meeting already this season, with Marske having dumped Shields out of the FA Cup back in September and also held them to a goalless draw in the league, but any thoughts of a tough afternoon were blown away inside the first 20 minutes as goals from Carl Finnigan and David Foley gave the home side a 2-0 lead that they never threatened to let slip.

It was a huge statement of intent from the Mariners, especially as seven days earlier, in front of more than 2,600 people, they'd lost 1-0 to rivals North Shields, fluffing their lines horribly in their biggest game of the season to date. For a while it looked like it would be a result which would come back to bite them on the backside in the latter stages of the campaign.

But for now, you could forget about the Jarrow March. This was the Mariners firmly pounding the streets to London.

CHAPTER TEN

A<small>PRIL</small> 18, 2017...

Woodhorn Lane, Ashington.

A new ground not yet steeped in the history that its predecessor, Portland Park, was but now a place etched into the history books of South Shields FC.

That Tuesday night in April will live long in the memory of the hundreds of Mariners fans who had made the long trip north, up the A19, to the famous old pit village that has more footballing connections than anywhere with a population so small has any right to have.

This is Ashington, birthplace of World Cup winners Bobby and Jackie Charlton and their cousin, former Newcastle United great Jackie Milburn.

The Northumberland town was back in the headlines in 2016 when Adidas released a limited edition trainer, the Adidas Ashington, in honour of the younger Charlton, Sir Bobby. They sold out within minutes despite their £90 price tag, with pairs swiftly appearing on eBay for £500.

Outside of that famous family, you had Burnley legend Jimmy Adamson, the man who turned down the England manager's job before Sir Alf Ramsey led them to World Cup glory, only to relegate Sunderland in 1976. Cec Irwin made more than 300 appearances for

Ipswich Town before ending his football career back at Ashington, while former Newcastle United defender Peter Ramage and ex-Blackburn and Birmingham stopper Martin Taylor were also born in the town. More recently, striker Mark Cullen scored the winning goal for Blackpool in their 2017 League Two play-off final at Wembley.

Nowadays, it is cricket that Ashington is just as closely associated with thanks to the pedigree and profile of Steve Harmison. The 'Ashington Express' became one of England's greatest fast bowlers, terrorising batsmen around the world with his pace and height, despite constantly yearning for his hometown with a home sickness which showed just how strong the pull of the region can be.

Harmison, for all his fame and wealth, never left Ashington. A strong sportsman and keen footballer, his family are now just as renowned in the town as the Charltons and Milburns were. Brother Ben joined him on Durham Cricket Club's books while the third sibling, James, became a strong club cricketer and a defender for Ashington.

In 2015, the football club hit the national headlines when they announced the appointment of Steve as their new manager. It was a bold move that signalled the ambition of the club's executive committee to not only raise the profile, but try to propel Ashington AFC back into the upper echelons of North East non-league football.

There are only a handful of Northern League clubs who could perhaps replicate the lift-off that South Shields have experienced over the last couple of years, and Ashington is one of those. The similarities between the two clubs is striking. Like Shields, Ashington used to play in the Football League; like Shields, they have a strong fanbase and an area that could be tapped into. The potential is huge for the Colliers, but so far hasn't been realised. The move to Woodhorn Lane in 2007 was hoped to be the kickstart the club needed after 37 years in the Northern League but so far, despite the best intentions of a strong and ambitious committee, it hasn't happened.

They still have the potential to attract big crowds. Woodhorn's record attendance is the 906 who crammed in to see Darlington 1883 play in 2013, though that was swelled by a significant away following as the phoenix club stormed to the Northern League title just 12 months after being reformed.

That 906 is still a far cry from the heady days at their former home, Portland Park. A huge, sprawling old stadium which had a dog track around it, Portland - originally named Station Road when Ashington first moved there in 1909 before being renamed in 1914 - had seen the best of times in the club's history. It had been Ashington AFC's home when they were elected into the new Third Division North of the Football League in 1921 as one of the founder members, alongside such teams as Stockport County, Darlington, Hartlepools (as they were known then), Wrexham, Wigan Borough, Durham City, Rochdale and Crewe Alexandra. Big clubs of today, such as Wolverhampton Wanderers and Derby County - both of whom would one day go on to become champions of England - also later joined the league, emphasising the strength and quality of teams at that level.

Ashington more than held their own under the leadership of player-manager Paddy O'Connell, a Dublin-born footballer who had starred for Manchester United among others in a varied career before landing in Northumberland in 1920. He guided them to 10th in their first season and it was a case of what might have been had they managed to keep hold of the Irishman. O'Connell was destined for bigger things, however, departing for the sunnier climes of Spain where he managed Racing de Santander to five regional titles before they became founding members of La Liga in 1928.

He later managed Real Betis to their one and only La Liga title to date, but perhaps his greatest claim to fame came as manager of Barcelona, whom he helped keep afloat during the Spanish Civil War when it looked like the financially-stricken club would go bust. O'Connell helped raise £5000 through taking the team on a tour of Mexico and the United States, money which ensured the Nou Camp outfit survived.

Back in Northumberland, without O'Connell Ashington still ticked along. In 1926-27 they reached the third round of the FA Cup, still their greatest run in the competition, before losing 2-0 to Nottingham Forest, but two years later they finished bottom of the

Third Division North and lost their bid for re-election, receiving just 14 votes compared to the 24 garnered by non-league York City.

Ashington remain the northernmost club to have played in the Football League but have never come close to getting back to those heights, unsuccessfully applying for election in 1947 (when no vote took place) and 1950 (when they received no votes). What 1950 did show, also though, was the undoubted potential of the club as 13,199 people piled into Portland Park to watch an FA Cup second round tie against Rochdale. It remains the club's record attendance.

They joined the Northern League in 1970 and have remained there ever since, both in the top flight and Division Two, with very little success. The ambition remains, however. Woodhorn Lane, a purpose-built ground, replaced the tired, crumbling Portland Park in 2007 and the main stand is a fantastic modern facility, among the best in the league.

It was in that big stand that Shields and Ashington fans both lingered to see if the Mariners could be crowned Northern League champions.

Shields had reached this point after a stunning run of victories which had hauled in North Shields when their rivals had looked set to gallop clear. At one point, the gap between the leaders and the Mariners was a mammoth 17 points, though Picton and Fenton's men still had six games in hand.

Catching up on those games, and without dropping points, was to be the biggest challenge. Out of their first 17 games of 2017, Shields played just five times in the league as cup competitions took precedence. It left the Mariners facing a hectic run-in of 10 games in 28 days, virtually all of which needed to be won if they were to land the title.

The first four of those came in a seven-day spell that included a season-defining win at Sunderland RCA. Shields had edged to a 2-1 win at Ryhope CW that included a jaw-dropping strike by Andrew Stephenson, then followed it up with a comfortable 4-0 win at home to Newton Aycliffe. Two days later, a Thursday night trip to RCA was to prove their biggest test yet.

At half-time, it was looking bleak for the visitors. A goal down and a man down after Alex Nicholson's dismissal two minutes before the break for an off-the-ball incident, Shields needed something special and once again they got it in the form of inspirational captain Arca.

The official website described the second-half performance as having come from a "team possessed" and it's hard to disagree with that description, but it was the little Argentinian who was the fulcrum. Arca hadn't started the game, rested to the bench as the management duo tried to rotate their squad but his introduction at half-time swung the game for Shields. Arca curled home a majestic free-kick for the equaliser and when Gavin Cogdon stabbed home the winner, Shields had a 28th successive victory.

The game was marred, though, by a sickening leg break for striker Stephen Ramsey, on as a substitute. It meant the long-serving star's season was over, just like the other club stalwart Leepaul Scroggins, meaning neither would be able to play at Wembley. For Ramsey, who had stuck with the club through the Peterlee days, showing incredible loyalty despite offers from elsewhere, and his family - Shields supporters through thick and thin - it was an undeserved blow.

Having used up all their replacements, Shields saw out 10 minutes of added time with just nine men for a thrilling three points that moved them eight behind North Shields with three games in hand. More than that, though, it showed this wasn't just a team of great footballers, but that they possessed the character and spirit needed when the chips are down.

Fenton and Picton both pinpoint that game as the highlight of the league run. Louis Storey's late winner a few weeks earlier in tough conditions at Newcastle Benfield also received an honourable mention, one of a number of single-goal victories that showed the team had a meanness in defence and an ability to take the big chance when it came along.

That was no more in evidence than at the Daren Persson Stadium on April 8. The top two sides finally met again and this time, it was South Shields who got the better of their North counterparts to record a 1-0 win that was notable for so many reasons.

On a sunny afternoon, the Mariners leapfrogged their rivals to the top of the table, sealing a top two spot and promotion in the process, after a stunning Foley strike which illustrated further his tendency to be the man for the big occasion. Again, Shields didn't make it easy though. Arca was sent off midway through the second half for two quick bookable offences and the Mariners, marshalled superbly by Shaw and goalkeeper Liam Connell, dealt comfortably with everything their title rivals could throw at them.

It was also, remarkably, a 31st consecutive victory, breaking the unofficial world record set by Scottish side East Kilbride the season before. It seemed nothing could halt this juggernaut and with promotion sealed, all they wanted now was the title.

It should have been clinched against Morpeth Town, only for the Highwaymen to get some modicum of revenge by claiming an injury-time equaliser at Mariners Park to put the champagne on ice and also end the winning run at 32.

It left Morpeth eight points behind Shields with three games left, as opposed to the Mariners' two. A win at Portland Park would still do the trick.

The queues for the little cafe snaked around the concourse as hundreds of Sand Dancers descended on Woodhorn in anticipation of seeing a little bit of history being made. Some of us were glad to have already had pizza beforehand, but would have to wait for the cuppa. Even on a balmy April evening, Ashington has an ever-present nip in the air.

There was plenty going on to warm the cockles, though. The Colliers' Barmy Army were in fine voice, their songs full of humour and good nature. They needed them, as it soon became apparent out on the pitch that there was only going to be one outcome.

Ashington had come into the game in the midst of a poor run of form. Any hope that Morpeth Town followers and players might have had about their neighbours doing them a favour and beating Shields would have disappeared exactly a week previously when the two Northumberland sides met themselves. That night, Morpeth had raced into a 3-0 lead inside 12 minutes, eventually running out easy 5-1 winners, and while South Shields weren't quite as quick out of the blocks, once they got their noses in front it was equally as comfortable.

Again, it was that man for the big occasion, David Foley, who settled any nerves, latching onto a quick throw-in from Robert Briggs to rifle home a volley past Conor Grant in the Ashington goal to give the Mariners a 12th-minute lead.

Within eight minutes, the title was won as the floodgates opened. Briggs split the woefully-square Ashington defence with a simple, yet superbly-executed through ball and Foley broke through, waltzed around Grant and virtually walked the ball into the back of the net. He could have even had time to make himself a cup of tea, such was the ease and space afforded him.

On 20 minutes, the title was sewn up and the celebrations could properly start amid more comical, kamikaze defending from the home side. Foley again caused confusion, Grant collided with one of his defenders as he tried to clear the ball on the edge of his box and Michael Richardson had the task of lofting the ball into an unguarded net from 30 yards.

Whatever Steve Harmison said to his players at half-time, it had an impact as the Colliers came out sharper and with more intensity. For a while in the second period, they were the better side and put the Shields goal under pressure. The Mariners, mind, had clearly taken their foot off the gas, preserving energy with three cup finals ahead of them. Changes were made, players rested, yet even with the extra pressure being exerted on them, they rarely looked like folding. Ashington did pull a goal back through Ryan McGorrigan, but it was little more than a consolation. Instead, the final word on a memorable night went to Cogdon. The little forward had been quiet most of the evening, but showed his class with the perfect finish in injury time to start the championship celebrations.

And celebrate they did, out on the pitch in front of that big stand which by now was packed with Mariners fans, creating an electric atmosphere, singing and dancing as the players congratulated each other out on the pitch and joined in the songs.

Afterwards, Picton spoke outside the changing rooms, delighted at finally lifting the championship, hunting down North Shields who had enjoyed that massive advantage at one point, holding off Morpeth's charge, doing it in style.

"I never got to a stage where I thought we were out of it.

"Even when we were 17 points behind I thought if there was any team that could go on a winning run like we needed to, then it was us.

"You cast your mind back to the halfway point which was the North Shields game, we were on 47 points after 21 games. We said to the lads that if we could better that in the second half of the season then we would have a great chance of getting promoted at the very least.

"It's been a monumental effort in the second half of the season. We've played 20 league games - won 19 and drawn one. You can't argue with that."

Up in the stand, as the players tucked into their post-match food there was no huge celebrations. Job done, on to the next game. Party time.

There had been no trophy out on the pitch at Woodhorn. Instead that would be presented at the final game of the season, down at Guisborough, where more than 750 Shields supporters made the 90-mile round trip to see their side lift the title for the first time, in what they also hoped would be the last Northern League game the club ever played.

It was anything but a drab end-of-season affair. Guisborough needed a win to secure Division One survival (they did eventually survive the drop, through a convoluted appeal to the Football Association in the summer) and it made for an entertaining affair.

Shields had made eight changes from the team that beat Ashington, with three cup finals on the horizon, but it took them just 100 seconds to break the deadlock. Harrison Scott - son of coach Martin - had been brought into the squad just before the deadline for signing new players but was making his debut in this game. He linked well with former Sunderland trainee Jordan Blinco, another late signing, who opened the scoring.

Guisborough quickly equalised through Steve Roberts but Barrie Smith restored the advantage with his first goal of the season, a fitting end to the league campaign for the stalwart who had been such an integral part of the club during the dark days.

Carl Finnigan made it 3-1 after the break and while Louis Goldsack pulled a late goal back for the home side, Guisborough couldn't spoil the Shields party. Fans piled on to the pitch as Leepaul Scroggins and Julio Arca lifted the trophy, presented to them by Northern League chairman Geoff Youngman and president George Courtney, the former FIFA referee who officiated in the 1986 and 1990 World Cups, but who started his career in the Northern League in the 1970s and remarkably, also ended it there. Having retired in 1992, just shy of his 51st birthday, he was called back into action on March 23, 2011 when with the referee and his replacement injured, he stepped out of the crowd to run the line to rapturous applause in the second half of the Northern League clash between Bishop Auckland and Billingham Synthonia. He was 69.

Courtney wasn't the main attraction this warm, sunny day, though. That was the men in the South Shields light blue change kit. Hundreds of pictures were taken alongside the cup, as players, officials and Geoff Thompson happily posed for photographs.

It was, up to that point, the greatest achievement in the Mariners' last 50 years.

There was even better to come, though.

CHAPTER ELEVEN

The league was in the bag and the FA Vase Final was still four weeks away but South Shields were not sitting idle for a month.

One down, three to go.

When the club had started the season, they were entered into five competitions. One of them they had no chance of winning, even with their fantastic squad. For all the resources at Geoff Thompson's disposal, the Mariners couldn't hope to compete with the hundreds of clubs above them in the pyramid when it came to the FA Cup.

Still, crashing out of the famous competition at the first hurdle was a blow but that 3-1 defeat to Marske on the opening day was to be the only cup game they lost all season.

Out of the FA Cup, there were still four competitions for the club to tackle. As well as the Northern League title and Vase, there was the Durham Challenge Cup and League Cup to be played for.

"In order of priority it was league, Vase then the other two," admitted Fenton. "But we just wanted to win games of football. It was the old classic cliche of just taking one game at a time, chalking another one off and moving on."

While securing promotion and getting to Wembley had been the main focuses, as momentum gathered over the course of the season it became evident that there was a real chance to do something special.

"We talked quite a lot to the players about legacy, saying it would be great if we won the league or great if we won the Vase but let's do something special this season, let's be part of the group that won the lot, the team that people will talk about in 10, 20, possibly 30 years time. Even if the club goes on to bigger and better things, there will still be people who say 'remember the 2016/17 season when we won the clean sweep'."

The Durham Challenge Cup is a prestigious trophy which dates back to 1884 when it was first competed for. Back then, it was won by Sunderland and the Black Cats still enter a team every year in the competition, though nowadays it is more a platform for their Under-23s or Under-18 players to gain experience of senior football.

The cup is open to all teams in the Durham County Football Association area, spreading far and wide geographically to take in the likes of Durham, Darlington, Hartlepool, Stockton-on-Tees, South Tyneside, Gateshead and Wearside.

Over the years, some massive clubs have lifted the old trophy. The professional teams in the area tend now to enter their reserve sides, but up against non-league players they are still a force to be reckoned with, as shown by Darlington Reserves' triumph in 2000, the win by Hartlepool United Reserves five years later, Sunderland Reserves in 2008 and Gateshead Reserves in 2011.

The strength of non-league football in the region, however, has meant many winners have come from the lower divisions, including some famous clubs with strong amateur pedigree. Between 1994 and 2002, eight of the nine finals were won by either Spennymoor or Bishop Auckland, who have both lifted the trophy a record 16 times in the various forms.

Success in recent years has been enjoyed by strong Northern League sides like Shildon, Consett and Billingham Synthonia, while the holders were Newton Aycliffe, who triumphed in the 2016 final with a 3-1 win over West Auckland.

That year's competition had been beset by controversy in the latter stages, with Shields at the heart of it. They had hosted Aycliffe in the semi-final at Mariners Park, as Jon King's in-form side that was sweeping all before them in Division Two came up against one of the toughest, most competitive sides in Division One.

In a hotly-contested and often controversial tie, Shields went 1-0 up through Julio Arca's penalty but it wasn't to be the last incident involving both Arca and spot kicks that night.

After Aycliffe battled back to go 2-1 up thanks to stunning strikes from Dennis Knight and Zak Boagey, a late equaliser by Shields defender Michael Turner sent the tie to extra time.

That was where it exploded. Arca had been involved in a long-running dispute with several Aycliffe midfielders, with the Mariners team and players feeling the former Sunderland man was being targeted by the opposition as they tried to put him off his game and ask questions about his temperament.

It paid off. Eight minutes before the end of extra time, Arca was sent off after the referee deemed he'd lashed out after an incident.

The South Shields official website described it thus: "Shields midfielder Arca had been involved in long-running confrontations with Aycliffe players, who appeared to be attempting to rile him using a number of tactics.

"On this occasion, when the ball had gone out of play and with both players on the ground, visiting substitute Neil Pattinson appeared to wrap his legs around Arca, preventing him from returning to his feet. This ensued for a number of seconds before Arca forced himself to his feet, pulling his leg away in the process. The referee saw Arca's actions as violent conduct and produced a red card, much to the disgust of the player and crowd."

Afterwards, there were allegations of certain remarks being made to Arca and talk of players having to be pulled away from each other in the bar after the game as tensions threatened to spill over again. It was an early indication, however, of how the opposition believed they could get to the Mariners' key man and playmaker and put him off his game by targeting that Latin temperament.

Shields managed to survive the last few minutes with 10 men to take the tie to penalties, but Aycliffe prevailed 3-1 in the shoot-out as Leepaul Scroggins saw his effort saved, Warren Byrne hit the crossbar and Robert Briggs blazed his effort over the crossbar to ensure a second cup exit on penalties after the Vase defeat earlier that season against Morpeth.

Aycliffe went on to the final where they were due to face Second

Division minnows Whickham, who had produced a remarkable run to the final to provoke memories of their 2006 triumph in the same competition as a Division Two side, when they had beaten several big names on the way. However, with just days to go before the final, Durham FA adjudged that Whickham had fielded an ineligible player as a late substitute in one of the earlier rounds, meaning Robin Falcus' side were expelled and West Auckland - who they had beaten in the semi-final - were given a reprieve.

There was no late reprieve for Shields, however, and their wait for Durham Challenge Cup glory would have to go on at least another year. The Mariners had lifted the trophy six times in their history, winning it for the first time in 1911 and then holding the trophy for half a decade after their 1914 success was the last time it was competed for until 1919 due to the outbreak of war. Further triumphs came in 1937, 1938 and 1949, but the final victory in 1977 meant success in the competition was long overdue.

Their bid began with a trip to Norton and Stockton Ancients in October. Shields were unbeaten in their 18 previous games, and headed into the encounter with the Division Two outfit on the back of beating Runcorn Linnets in the Vase. Managers Picton and Fenton shuffled the pack with the likes of Arca, Scroggins and Gavin Cogdon unavailable, but they weren't missed as defender Dillon Morse scored his first two goals for the club, David Carson powered home a third and another defender, Ben Riding, added a fourth to complete a comfortable night's work.

The second round pitted Shields up against neighbours and old foes Jarrow Roofing for their first game of 2017. Having hammered their local rivals 5-0 in the league earlier in the season, many expected an easy passage but it was a tight affair as two much-changed teams blew off the New Year cobwebs.

Cogdon was making his first start in two months after a bad groin injury, and he fired the Mariners in front before Carl Finnigan added the second. Tom Bailey grabbed an injury-time consolation for Roofing but it was a 10th successive win for Shields.

The game was also notable, in hindsight, for the appearance of Scroggins, captaining the side on his own return from injury. The 45 minutes he played was to be his last start in a first-team shirt for the club. The day after he'd made a brief cameo in the next game, playing a few minutes as a substitute before the lights went out against Morpeth, the midfielder broke his leg playing Sunday football in a bid to regain some match sharpness. It ruled him out for the rest of the season, a devastating end to his Shields career for a man who had made more than 200 appearances for the club. However, it was not to be his last involvement with the Mariners and in the summer he was asked to take the reins of the reserve team, bringing in old pal and former Shields star David Graham as his No 2. Anyone who saw the pair of them out on the pitch wouldn't want to criticise their tactics in the dressing room.

Without Scroggins, Shields moved on to face Hartlepool United for a place in the Durham Challenge Cup semi-finals. Jon Shaw was shifted back up front and rolled back the years to nod home the opener on 22 minutes and add further weight to some people's perception that he should still be playing as a striker.

In Shaw's place in the centre of defence was new signing Darren Lough. The former Newcastle United academy prospect had been added to the squad a few days later after his international clearance came through, the defender having spent two seasons playing in Iceland with KA Akureyri.

He'd have felt right back at home with the icy temperatures at Mariners Park that night, but Shields were able to warm their fans' hearts with two stunning goals after the break which sealed a 3-0 win. Anthony Callaghan blasted home his first goal for the club via the underside of the crossbar, and Briggs' free kick crossed the line in a similar fashion as a young Pools side, which still featured several first-team players like Kenton Richardson, Nicky Deverdics, Jordan Richards and Devante Rodney, had no answer to the Mariners' steam train.

For the second year in succession, Shields were in the semi-finals but this time they were determined to go one step further. Consett stood in their way, hosting the Mariners at their fantastic Belle View Stadium where their 4G pitch, burgeoning crowds and healthy youth set-up were seen as a model for many Northern League clubs to follow.

Three days before the clash, Shields had set a new club record with a 21st successive win as they beat fellow title-chasers Shildon 2-0 and any worries over whether playing on an artificial surface would hinder their bid to make it 22 in a row were quickly dispelled on a night that saw sensational goals and one world-class save.

Having weathered an early storm, Shields went in front on eight minutes with a lovely goal from Andrew Stephenson, who was starting to show the form that had prompted Picton and Fenton to bring him in from Spennymoor.

Then came that save. Trying to do it justice in print is an almost impossible task so once you've read these words, get on to YouTube and search for Peter Jeffries. The Consett goalkeeper was facing his own net when Cogdon side-footed the ball into a gaping goal from four yards out, only for Jeffries to somehow, incredibly, not only get his right-hand to the ball but then scoop and flick it over his shoulder in one action.

It was an astonishing save and the camera behind the goal captured it perfectly. Before long, the footage had gone viral, shown on Sky Sports, Fox News in America and all around the world as flabbergasted viewers tried to make sense of the 'save of the century'.

Anything Warren Byrne can do…

Speaking of Byrne, spare a thought for Carl Finnigan too. His goal, a few minutes later, had echoes of Byrne's famous strike but in the aftermath of Jeffries' wonder save, didn't get as much credit as it perhaps should have done. The forward received the ball 30 yards from goal, backheeled it into Cogdon and then spun behind a defender to receive his strike partner's first-time pass back. As the ball dropped over his left shoulder, Finnigan hit a left-foot volley which arced and dipped over Jeffries, who this time was helpless to stop Shields from doubling their lead.

It was to be Finnigan and Cogdon's last real involvement as the number of games, and perhaps the artificial pitch, took their toll. Both were forced off with injuries to leave the management duo sweating on their fitness with some big games coming up.

Stephenson sealed their passage through to the final with a third goal just after the restart and despite a Consett consolation, it was another memorable night for Shields, leaving their fans dreaming of more silverware.

That victory over Consett was the first of four successive semi-final ties for the Mariners. Ten days later came the first leg of the Vase semi-final at Coleshill, followed by the return fixture, and the sequence was rounded off with a trip to Shildon in the last four of the League Cup.

Unlike the Durham Challenge Cup, Shields had tasted more recent success in the League Cup. Under Gary Steadman's stewardship, they had won the competition back in 2010 as they began to establish themselves as a top flight Northern League team, having been promoted two years earlier. Shields beat Ashington, managed by Gary Middleton, on penalties after a 2-2 draw to lift silverware for the first time in 15 years, and their first trophy as a Northern League side.

It was the highlight of Steadman's successful spell as manager. Another who was South Shields born and bred, he'd taken over with the club on the verge of extinction and struggling at the foot of Division Two. Remarkably, in his first full season in charge Steadman propelled them to promotion in 2008 on the back of some fantastic nights at Filtrona Park, and then guided the club to their highest league placing in more than a decade, before stepping down the following season after a crushing FA Vase exit at the hands of Billingham Town.

The League Cup win had shown the potential of the club to compete with some of the bigger teams in the division, and also the quality players coming out of South Tyneside. Made up largely of local players, the likes of skipper Scroggins - who scored a late equaliser in the final to send the game to extra time - Stephen Ramsey, David Graham and Jonny Wightman were all part of the side that lifted the trophy.

THE SIDE of 2016/2017 was a different proposition, with some of the best non-league players from across the region assembled together, though there were still a handful of South Tynesiders in the midst, as illustrated as Shields launched their League Cup bid with a home tie against Blyth Town.

Ramsey skippered the side that day on a rare start, and with the likes of the Carson brothers, Wayne Phillips and adopted Sand Dancer Barrie Smith in the starting line-up, along with Simon Parkin and Carl Finnigan, plus youngsters Danny Barlow and Ryan Bolam on the bench, there was a strong South Shields flavour running throughout the team.

There was one more Sand Dancer in the starting line-up, though, and his impact was to be decisive. David Foley produced a stunning individual performance to see off Blyth, as he netted all four goals in a virtuoso display of forward play in a 4-2 win. It was much-needed, with Shields having trailed 2-1 at one stage to the ambitious Division Two outfit, and having seen David Carson miss a penalty.

Shields had to wait almost two months before their next tie in the competition, disposing of Penrith 4-1 in their third round clash. The result was a replica of the scoreline when the two teams had met on Boxing Day in the league and was most notable for a thunderous strike from fully 30 yards by Romanian defender Iulian Petrache.

That set up a quarter-final at Newcastle Benfield, a game which was bound to test the mettle of this Shields team. And the runaway train was almost derailed. That it wasn't was down to the most surprising twist in an incident-packed night at Sam Smiths Park, when Benfield's veteran striker Paul Brayson missed a late penalty to send the game into extra time.

Games at this point were coming thick and fast for the Mariners, and at times on a wet and miserable Wednesday night they struggled to get their passing game going on a soggy pitch that was cutting up in several places. Adapting to the conditions, however, they took the lead through Michael Richardson, whose goal threat from midfield was becoming an increasingly potent weapon in their artillery.

There has arguably never been a bigger goal threat in Northern League football over the last 20 years than Brayson, however. A former Newcastle United youngster, he acquired a reputation as a fearsome goalscorer at reserve-team level in the mid-1990s, but was perhaps in the wrong place at the wrong time while with the Magpies as he saw his chances of breaking into the first team halted by having the likes of Alan Shearer, Les Ferdinand, Peter Beardsley & Co in his way. Progress was hampered further by Kevin Keegan's astonishing decision to scrap the reserve team in protest at the FA's insistence that a percentage of games be played at St James' Park and from breaking all sorts of goalscoring records at youth and reserve-team level, Brayson found his pathway to the first team at Newcastle blocked.

He made just one start for his hometown team - a Coca Cola Cup tie against Bristol City - before a successful loan spell at Swansea City eventually helped earn him a £100,000 move to Reading and then another move to Cardiff City, where he showed he could transfer that golden touch into senior football.

It was in non-league, however, that he really made his mark, becoming one of the most feared strikers outside the Football League. A goal-laden spell at Northwich Victoria ended with him returning to the North East where he continued his feats in front of goal with the likes of York City, Gateshead, Blyth Spartans and Bedlington Terriers before moving to Benfield for the 2013/14 season. In every season since joining, he has bagged more than 40 goals, an astonishing feat of penalty-box prowess which showed his ability, agility, reflexes and sharpness haven't dulled despite the advancing years.

Brayson, as usual, was a constant threat against Shields, only a combination of last-ditch defending and good goalkeeping denying him an equaliser.

The game looked to have finally swung Shields' way, though, when Benfield defender Stephen Tobin was sent off with just over 20 minutes to go, but rather than being the point where the tie was killed off, it saw the game ignite. Brayson was inches wide with a header before he finally grabbed the goal he'd been threatening. Latching on to a ball over the top with 13 minutes to go, he was hauled down in the penalty area by Morse, who was sent off himself. Brayson picked himself up and coolly slotted the ball past Liam Connell for the equaliser.

Game on. Both teams were down to 10 men and searching for a winner, and Shields rose to the challenge. There were four minutes left on the clock when Richardson raced through on to Cogdon's pass, rounded the goalkeeper and tucked away his second goal of the night.

Game over. Well, not quite. There was still time for one last twist as Benfield went straight back down the other end and were awarded a penalty after Alex Nicholson's handball. Brayson stepped up but proved he was fallible after all as he thumped his effort against the crossbar.

In a season where you are going for four trophies, you won't get there without having a little bit of luck. Brayson finished that campaign with 53 goals from 52 appearances but it was the one that got away which was all that mattered to South Shields.

That put the Mariners into the last four of the competition and a meeting with Shildon. Played three days after the second-leg Vase tie against Coleshill, Picton and Fenton rang the changes, using their squad to the maximum effect. A couple of weeks earlier, Sunderland AFC youngster Jordan Blinco had been signed, and this was to be the highlight of his brief stay at the club. The forward had travelled down to Coleshill for the first game, but cut an isolated figure at times, ineligible to play and new to the squad. However, handed his debut in the semi-final, he was the central character in a 4-1 triumph that secured a hat-trick of cup final appearances for the Mariners.

It hadn't started well for Shields. Five minutes into the game at Dean Street, the home side went ahead through Michael Rae and it would have been interesting to see how the Mariners would have fared had Shildon then not had captain Jamie Harwood sent off just seven minutes later.

The incident was controversial to say the least, but came after a typically patient build-up from Shields which saw a dozen passes exchanged across the back four and through midfield before Alex Nicholson burst from midfield and squared the ball for Blinco, who looked set to tap home into a gaping goal, only for Harwood to deny him with what appeared to be a great saving tackle. The referee saw differently, however, pointing to the spot and then compounding Shildon's anger by flashing the red card to the infuriated Harwood, who must have detested playing against Shields by this point, having also been dismissed in the league game between the two teams earlier in the season.

Finnigan stepped up to rifle home the resultant penalty and while the scores were still level at the interval, the game was almost up for Shildon.

After the half-time interval, Blinco - having created the equaliser for his strike partner - saw the favour repaid as Finnigan nodded down for him to put Shields ahead and bar an excellent save from Connell to deny Rae a breakaway equaliser, the Mariners were in cruise control.

It can be hard enough playing against Shields with 11 men but with a player light, it often became a case of chasing shadows for the home side and the biggest competition on the night ended up being the verbal battle on the terraces, with the travelling Shields fans drowning out the cries of 'where were you at Peterlee?' and 'where were you when you were shit?' from the Shildon faithful.

On the pitch, Blinco continued to make an impact by rifling home a third goal before Finnigan wrapped up the win with a fourth, looping home a header, and both forwards went close to hat-tricks in the latter stages as a 25th straight win set up a cup final against North Shields.

At this stage, North Shields had a whopping 17-point gap at the top of the table, and with South Shields facing a fixture backlog as well as having three cup finals on the horizon, the Robins must have fancied their chances of winning the title, if not a league and cup double.

But by the time the two sides met just over six weeks later, the momentum was fully with the side south of the Tyne. By then, South Shields had not only won nine out of their last 10 league games inside 28 days to overhaul their rivals, including that crucial 1-0 win at the Daren Persson Stadium, but North Shields were in the midst of a minor crisis.

Turning up to the League Cup Final at Whitley Bay's Hillheads home, the buzz around the famous old ground was not about whether North Shields could stop the juggernaut, but instead concerned Robins manager John McDonald having been told a couple of days before the game that he was being sacked.

McDonald had taken the reins at North Shields after Fenton's departure across the Tyne in September and had done a phenomenal job. Against most expectations, he'd kept the team competing at the top of the table with a steady hand on the tiller, winning game after game when many had believed they would falter. Their final tally of 101 points had only been bettered twice in a 42-game season in the previous 10 years, and with a cup final still to come, it seemed McDonald had done an incredible job.

Not so much in the eyes of the North Shields committee, it seemed. Rumours were rife before kick-off that McDonald had been told the cup final would be his final game in charge and that player power had played a big part in his axing.

Once kick-off came, the players did little to dispel that rumour. They may have been right behind their manager, but it didn't look like it as the Mariners tore into them from the start.

Fenton knew that squad better than most, having built it up over a four-year period, and he admitted something just didn't feel right about the contest.

"There was a funny atmosphere, just speaking to a few of the North Shields lads before the game. There was a lot of uncertainty in their camp at the time."

South Shields capitalised, in part due to Fenton's knowledge of how their opponents would be set up and in part due to the lack of focus, energy and application from their rivals. Who can tell whether it had been the demands of a long season taking their toll, the disappointment of seeing the league title slip from their grasp, or the effect of that crunch defeat in the league just four weeks earlier, or even the uncertainty surrounding the manager situation?

But one thing is for sure, this was a different North Shields team to that which produced a sterling backs-to-the-wall, defiant, committed display at Mariners Park earlier that season when they became the last side to defeat South Shields.

Less than five minutes were on the clock when the Mariners were ahead with a goal that epitomised what was to come. Gavin Cogdon was electric all game, but was allowed time and space to get his shot away as North Shields' defenders backed off and off, with the ball eventually looping over Kyle Hayes to send South Shields on their way.

The second goal, just eight minutes later, was straight off the training ground. An inswinging corner from Nicholson found Shaw -

who had crept across the six-yard box without being picked up - unmarked at the front post and his header crept over the line despite the efforts of Hayes to keep it out.

It was a personal triumph for Fenton, whose attention to detail at set-pieces paid dividends again.

"I liked that goal because you have to remember, I set North Shields up in that formation at set-pieces to be zonal, so we did a set-piece to exploit the zonal system," he said. "It was great delivery and Shawsy's obviously got on the end of it and that was a pleasing moment."

Thirteen minutes in and the game was all but done. North Shields were demoralised and their body language revealed it. Finnigan went close to a third just 30 seconds after the restart but it was Cogdon who made it 3-0 on 33 minutes, out-thinking and outpacing the usually ultra-reliable Robins skipper Kevin Hughes to score.

The day was to get even worse for Hughes and North Shields. They somehow survived without conceding further until half-time as Cogdon went close to another but the little striker did get his hat-trick after the break when Finnigan was brought down in the box and handed over penalty duties to his strike partner, who duly converted, before being confronted by a pitch invader who took umbrage to his celebrations.

It was one of a couple of unsavoury scenes, including objects being thrown over the fence at South Shields fans in the first half, though my attention was distracted by being stuck in a huge queue for the toilets. Nothing was going to distract South Shields however, nor spoil their day, and when Finnigan rattled home a long-range effort before the end to make it 5-0, it was the biggest margin of victory in the final of the competition in 58 years.

"It was just a really pleasing performance on not a great pitch," said Fenton. "We played some great football, some great stuff and on the day we were just far too good for them."

The celebrations were lengthy, both on the pitch after the presentation as hundreds of fans poured off the terraces to congratulate the players and pose for pictures, and then in the dressing room afterwards. It had been a comfortable win, more comfortable than most had expected, but with the uncertainty and rumours around the North Shields camp before the game, perhaps that shouldn't have been unexpected.

"It was a strange one," admitted Picton. "But in the changing room together, the group photo together with the champagne and trophy, we knew there was just one more step to go and that we had something incredible."

There was one more step because just three days earlier, Shields had sealed their second trophy of the season, lifting the Durham Challenge Cup with another straightforward and comfortable win in a final.

Up against Billingham Synthonia at Hartlepool United's Victoria Park, Shields produced a competent, professional performance to see off their opponents, who had enjoyed a fantastic season of their own to gain promotion from Division Two as well as reach the cup final.

They'd not had it easy along the way, knocking out some big teams to progress through the ranks, none more so than Hartlepool Reserves in their second game of the competition, winning 2-1, having beaten Sunderland RCA in the first round.

Another fantastic scalp came in the form of Shildon, who were defeated on penalties 2-1, while a third top-flight side were beaten with a narrow semi-final success over Newton Aycliffe.

The final, however, was a step too far for Synners. Their star man, Macaulay Langstaff, had earned a move to Gateshead with his displays that season but he couldn't sign off with a goal as he was restricted to few opportunities to shine by the tough Mariners defence.

Synners held their own for the majority of the first half as Shields struggled at times to find their rhythm, but once Andrew Stephenson opened the scoring five minutes before the interval, there was only going to be one winner.

Stephenson celebrated with a knee slide in front of the huge South Shields following in the large Niramax stand that stood opposite the dugouts. His goal was reward for an excellent first-half display on the right side of the midfield diamond, and Stephenson's performance that evening - along with some of his displays in the couple of weeks previous - sealed his place in the starting line-up at Wembley.

"It was his best spell at the club by a country mile, that last month, six weeks of the season," said Picton. "That goal he scored against Ryhope was out of this world and his general level of performance was brilliant to the point where the biggest decision we had to make ahead of the Vase final was either Robert Briggs or Andrew Stephenson."

Against Synners, Briggs was given his opportunity to shine at the base of the diamond in the absence of Arca, who was suspended after his red card in the league game against North Shields some three weeks previous. Briggs performed well, showing his versatility, but Stephenson's level had increased a notch and he was to get the nod.

After the break, Foley quickly added a second on the ground where he had enjoyed so many happy memories as a youngster with Hartlepool. He still holds the record as the youngest player in the club's history, and while his tap-in from four yards won't rank at all in his list of greatest goals, it gave him plenty of pleasure because of where it was scored.

Shields should have added further goals to the tally that night, but a 2-0 scoreline and a second trophy of the season was all that mattered and the celebrations in front of the big crowd were well received.

"It was a good performance," said Fenton. "To get to Victoria Park, the ground was decent, the crowd was unbelievable. To look across and see that far stand full was amazing.

"The lads put on a really strong performance. It goes without saying that we were almost in cruise control in that second half, it was that easy."

Two easy cup final wins in the space of three days, but the scorelines were only so comfortable because of the focus and dedication the squad had shown, driven on by the management duo. It would have been easy for them to take their eye off the ball at some point with the league won and an appearance at Wembley on the horizon. Not once, however, during that last month of the season was there any sign of players looking to protect themselves, pulling out of tackles or having one eye on the Vase final.

Picton and Fenton both preached the old mantra of 'one game at a time' to keep players grounded but also used motivational techniques to retain the focus and let everyone know there were still 11 spots at Wembley up for grabs.

The tactics board, used every game, was used as a tactic itself. Positioned in the centre of the dressing room for every game, Fenton and Picton set their formation out every game but then also left question marks over each position as a motivation that the players could still win a place in the Vase final.

"We had that in the dressing room and it was there for everyone to see before every game," said Picton. "That period from winning the Vase semi-final to the final itself was about two months and we used that board to say, 'there's the team for Wembley, who is going to play in it?'"

Finnigan stepped up, and so did Stephenson. While the romantic decision, made from the heart, may have been to play Briggs who had performed so well over the season, Stephenson was undoubtedly the man in form.

"Rightly or wrongly, we felt we had to stick to our guns," said Picton. "We'd been repeating the same message all the time: the performances you'd put in three, four, five months ago count for nothing now, you've got to put your name on that board between now and the end of the season."

It's a point Fenton is keen to expand on. "Robert played a lot of games. He carries a knee injury, he's still carrying it, and over the length of the season it was giving him jip more and more towards the end and you could see it in some of his performances."

Any regrets over the decision? For once, the two managers aren't in complete agreement.

"In hindsight, it was the wrong decision," says Picton. "Absolutely."

Fenton: "Nah, I disagree. On the information we had it wasn't the wrong decision."

"In hindsight, it was wrong," clarifies Picton. "Andrew was poor in the final and I'd be willing to bet my mortgage we'd have got more out of Briggsy. But you're right Graham, we felt we had to make that decision because of how we'd built up that process between the Vase semi-final and the final. But you can't get everything right."

If the only decision they got wrong in a season was the selection of one player in a final which they comfortably won 4-0, then most South Shields fans will probably forgive them.

CHAPTER TWELVE

Where do you go from lifting four trophies in one season?

Where do you go from a historic Wembley win?

In the immediate aftermath, it was back to the team hotel for the Shields players.

Eventually.

While things are done as professionally as possible on the pitch, and around the club in general, there are still constant reminders of how far football club has come in a short space of time. After their post-match food in Wembley Stadium itself, the players - at the insistence of club captain Scroggins - wanted to meet up with friends, family and fans for a couple of drinks before heading back to the hotel, so made their way to the Green Man pub a quarter of a mile outside the ground.

It was a perfect day for drinking outside, even clothed in a three-piece suit and the Green Man is famous for being the venue for football fans to congregate pre-match and post-match to celebrate or commiserate. Mainly the latter, if you're a Newcastle or Sunderland supporter.

For the Mariners, it was definitely the former and with the sun beating down, the players mingled with well-wishers to toast the culmination of an astonishing campaign.

When it was finally time to depart back to the hotel, however, there was a problem. The two coaches - one for the team, the other for family - couldn't get near the pub or stadium because of road closures. Messages were sent via Graham Fenton, on board one of the buses, to his managerial partner Lee Picton for the players to walk this way, then that way, to try and find a location where the bus could pick everyone up. There was plenty grumbling among the players while seeing Carl Finnigan, shoes off because of blisters, treading the Wembley pavements, along with the rest of the squad, including Stephen Ramsey on crutches, was a strange sight. All the way back to the stadium, then a turn around and halfway back to the pub, until just as the final whistle had sounded in the game that followed the FA Vase (a 3-2 FA Trophy win for York City), the coaches were found.

"I bet Manchester United never had this problem," quipped one wag as the players lined up at an ice cream van on Wembley Way while they waited for the bus driver to find them.

It's easy to forget, sometimes, that this is a non-league club, still heavily reliant on a group of unpaid volunteers, a hardy bunch of fans who just want to be part of their community club. South Shields FC isn't a multi-billion pound company like the Manchester Uniteds and Liverpools of this world. It is an amateur club, now playing in the seventh tier of English football against sides whose budget can be as little as £20,000 per year.

Shields had a much larger expenditure than that, and larger than just about every Northern League club they were up against, though there were some other high-spenders in the league such as Morpeth and Shildon. Around £5,500 a week was spent on average through the season on the playing staff. That's more than £280,000 in the season, a whopping figure which blows most other teams at that level out of the water. In contrast, Whickham, who finished sixth in Division Two the same season, spent just £9,000 on players throughout the entire campaign.

So while not professional, the Mariners aren't far away, a fact recognised by chairman Thompson.

"We need to be running the club on a professional basis," he said. "The commercial model, the right financial control and reporting, the right IT, it all has to be done on a professional level. There then becomes the point at where does the first team become full-time professionals but we haven't got a timetable for that, it's too early. What we need to do is to get through another two or three promotions and knocking on the door of the Conference, but why not?"

Already a number of full-time employees work at the club, a far cry from the Peterlee days when that stout band of volunteers kept the club afloat in their spare time. Crutwell had been rewarded for his dedication and support by being offered the role of site manager/groundsman at Mariners Park, running the place on a day-to-day basis. Alisha Henry was appointed as marketing manager while Geoff's daughter, Steph, was part of the club board and organised many of the operations until going on maternity leave.

In the aftermath of Wembley, further big decisions were made. Managing director Mike Orr left the club, replaced by Keith Finnigan, while David Mitchell came on board as commercial director and Rachel Sarginson was appointed as operations director in a boardroom shuffle that showed Thompson wasn't content with how the club was running.

The biggest full-time appointments, however, were those of Fenton and Picton.

A fortnight before the big day at Wembley, Shields announced that the duo would be leaving their roles at Monkseaton High School, in North Tyneside, where they had overseen the football academy there, to cross the Tyne and take up full-time roles at South Shields, not just as first-team managers but also launching a new academy at Mariners Park.

As Thompson described it, this was a 'landmark step' for the club and unheard of at this level. Professional clubs around them - Newcastle, Sunderland, Middlesbrough - all have their own academies, while National League outfit Gateshead also assist their full-time model with an education programme linked in with the town's college.

In an ambitious, exciting move, Shields had decided to take the plunge and set up their own academy for 16-19-year-olds. Capped at

40 over the Under-17, Under-18 and Under-19 range, to preserve its elite nature, it was announced the academy coaching would be carried out by Lee and Graham in conjunction with the Improtech Soccer Elite coaching company run by former Sunderland AFC star Martin Scott, while the education element for A-Level, Btec and HND courses would be provided by Sunderland College.

"Obviously the relationships we've established through Lee and Graham with the likes of Martin Scott at Improtech and latterly Sunderland College means that we've got the right parties involved to create something that is quite unique," said Thompson.

"Each of the parties are bringing something to the table and all of that is part of that overall investment. Frankly, from a profit and loss view it doesn't work, but you have to take a long-term view. The idea is that if you've got up to 40 students in the South Shields academy and you can develop and nurture that talent then eventually some of that talent, we hope, will end up playing first-team football for South Shields.

"Some of it might end up going even further or might move into other clubs. But the idea is to create quite a unique academy with the parties, have the right talent, develop that talent then hopefully nurture that talent so it feeds into the first team.

"It's happened sooner than I imagined but in life, sometimes things come together and an opportunity presents itself. In our case it was a football club that had relative success over the last couple of years, the arrival of Lee and Graham, the relationship with Improtech Soccer and Martin, and more latterly the new relationship with the college.

"We could have passed that by, we could have done nothing but I think in life it's true to say there are moments where it's the right thing to do. Timing. You can plan these things until you're blue in the face but ultimately it comes down to all of these things coming together at the right time and then making the decision that 'right, I may not have imagined this was going to happen this soon, but there's a great opportunity to do something so let's make it happen'.

"We are going to have a very close-knit academy. Lee and Graham are passionate about understanding their players, those students, so that it's not just a numbers game and every one of those students is going to be properly looked after both from a footballing perspective, a personal development perspective but of course their academic development as well. It's a lot more focused and dedicated set-up that we will have, which will differentiate what we do with what some of the larger academies do in the larger football clubs up there in the Premier League.

"One could argue that when you've got hundreds of kids going through those programmes, sadly very few of them get into first-team football. What we are hoping is that because ours is more close-knit, more focused, with a lot more personal attention - we haven't got any aspirations to grow it to hundreds of students - for those reasons it will be different."

It was a huge development for the club. Having full-time managers on board, who also run an academy set-up that they hope will mirror what is happening at professional clubs, was an absolute statement of intent about where Thompson wants South Shields to be in a short period of time, and the faith he has invested in Picton and Fenton.

The pair had vast experience of running the football academy at Monkseaton. For them, it seemed a natural progression to align what they do in their day jobs with what they want to achieve, alongside the chairman, at Mariners Park.

"It's fully in line with the ambitions the club has shown consistently across the board," Picton explained. "The club has never tried to hide the fact that it wants to get to a level of full-time football and this is just another piece in the jigsaw.

"We've amassed such a wealth of experience and different skills through our time at Monkseaton. We're very proud of the success we've achieved at Monkseaton on a national level across a number of years. What we've got the opportunity to do here is to bring that experience across, bring those skills across but also be able to take things to the next level up from there because of what you're able to do being based at a football club.

"We're not a professional football club YET but that doesn't put any limitations or boundaries on how we run the academy. Our focus will be on running the 16-19-year-olds just like a professional academy will be run. That's the aim and something we're really confident of being able to do."

Fenton can call on his experience as a professional footballer, learning the ropes at Aston Villa on the old-school YTS programmes before academies became the norm at pro clubs. It served him well, and it's an experience he wants to deliver to young students - with South Shields FC also benefiting.

"I had a great time. I was spoilt rotten at Aston Villa with some fantastic coaching from Richard Money for the first two years and then stepping into the reserves and playing with some exceptionally talented players.

"The ethos of the club developed me as a person, that real work ethic and being a team player and that's what Lee and myself pride ourselves on saying to the lads at South Shields.

"There may be opportunities for lads in our 16-19 programme to step into the first team if lads can't do the travel and sometimes you just need that lucky break. I had it at a very early age with Aston Villa at 19 years of age. I went out on loan and did quite well at West Brom, then came back and went straight into the first team at Aston Villa and was fortunate to play at Wembley in my fourth game.

"I had a fantastic time and that's ultimately what we're trying to do with our programme here - give the lads an experience of enjoying themselves and learning what is needed to be a good footballer. Not just in terms of technique but tactically, mentally.

"We used video analysis at Monkseaton for years - looking at all levels of the game, Barcelona, Swansea City, working down the leagues. We showed footage of South Shields to the Monkseaton lads and it's really beneficial because if you can show a 16 or 17-year-old kid a Barcelona game I don't know if they can quite see themselves getting there but if you show them a South Shields first team game and how it looks and how the team plays together, they can almost visualise themselves getting there in a short period of time."

Picton agrees, especially with the opportunity having the academy can afford both students and the clubs when it comes to the first team.

He said: "There are going to be times when there's a long away trip that some of your first team squad are going to struggle to make because of work commitments and that might open up a few opportunities at a very early stage for some of our more talented 16-19s to step up.

"But the bigger aim is to produce players who are going to be regulars in the first team. We're confident with the level of contact time we are going to have with these lads over a two or three-year period that we can develop some seriously talented footballers. If they don't go on to play for the first team here at South Shields then we hope they go on and play at a really good standard somewhere else."

South Tyneside has been littered with talented footballers over the years. Many came through the old Jarrow-based Monkton Youth League or the Russell Foster Youth League, still going strong from its Newbottle base. In recent years, they've been snapped up by the big boys, however. Newcastle United took Carl Finnigan and Richard Offiong, who both had good careers in Scotland after serving their apprenticeships with the Magpies. Jamie Chandler, Martyn Waghorn and Blair Adams are recent graduates from the Academy of Light down the road at Cleadon.

Left-back Adams starred for the likes of Coventry City and Notts County after leaving Sunderland, while England Under-21 international Waghorn cost Leicester City a couple of million pounds before finding home at the mighty Rangers, where his goalscoring exploits helped them back up the leagues and into the SPL, and himself a move back to England with Ipswich.

Chandler had a successful spell in Sunderland's reserves before being a key member of Gateshead's fantastic side that got to Wembley for the first time in their history in 2014. There he played in midfield alongside another South Tynesider, Phil Turnbull, who along with twin brother Stephen had begun their careers at Hartlepool. As had David Foley, still Pools' youngest-ever player at just 16 years and 105 days.

So much talent to tap into. If Shields can capture some of these youngsters in their academy, the long-term future of the club could be safeguarded.

"I was talking to a gentleman who owns a very successful Conference side and their wage bill is significant," said Thompson.

"Then on top of the wage bill you have any transfer fees to bring in talent at that level. So I think while we will obviously have to bring in new talent over time, it's about a combination of things. The idea is that the academy will be developing local talent and nurturing that, giving the lads a good education but also some great football coaching and development and all of the curriculum and academic side is delivered by the college.

"The young lads are getting some good education, training and development but from a South Shields perspective we are investing in that future talent."

It paid off quickly. When Shields played their Integro Cup semi-final against Evo-Stik Premier Division side Coalville Town in April of the following season, the starting XI contained four academy players with another couple on the bench, further proof that the future looks bright for the Mariners.

CHAPTER THIRTEEN

APRIL 28, 2018...

A familiar picture.

Julio Arca lifts aloft the trophy, players around him celebrating as fans cheer on.

Some of the faces are different, but the majority are those who picked up four similar bits of silverware 12 months earlier.

The Mariners had taken the Evo-Stik North division by storm. Another league championship, another century of points on the board. Three titles, three promotions, three 100-plus points tallies on the board.

Most clubs had expected Shields to breeze through the league and in the end, they were comfortable winners, finishing eight points ahead of runners-up Scarborough Athletic and 11 ahead of third-placed Hyde United. The top two teams gained automatic promotion and the other two clubs had kept Shields on their toes throughout the season. The margin between the Mariners and their rivals had been wide by the end of the campaign, but it certainly hadn't been the walk in the park many had predicted.

There had been a slight wobble over the festive period. A 2-2 draw at home to Trafford two days before Christmas was followed by a Boxing Day stalemate at Kendal Town. When Scarborough - a former Football League side themselves, with designs on returning to the big time - left Mariners Park with a 3-1 win on New Year's Day, it was three games without a win for Shields. A blip by most club's standards, but having grown accustomed to seeing them win virtually every game over the last two years, it set a few pulses racing.

Normal service was quickly resumed with wins over Tadcaster Albion, Mossley and then before January was out, a superb 3-0 win at home to promotion rivals Hyde United. There was to be just one more league defeat the rest of the season - a midweek 3-2 loss at Bamber Bridge - a setback that the team quickly bounced back from, scoring 19 goals in their next four games to all but clinch promotion.

That eventually arrived on April 17 with a 3-0 home win over Glossop North End. Carl Finnigan opened the scoring after 40 seconds and his erstwhile strike partner Gavin Cogdon sealed the win with two further goals as Shields celebrated a third successive promotion.

Finnigan was to end the season as top goalscorer, with Cogdon not far behind him, as the pair led the line for most parts of the season in the absence of David Foley, whose shock departure just a couple of weeks after the Wembley win had stunned the club. Foley had rejected a new deal at Mariners Park, tempted instead by the deal on offer at Spennymoor Town who were hoping to have a real go at the National League North.

While promotion was comfortably achieved in the end, Foley was undoubtedly a big miss throughout the season. No South Shields player finished in the top 10 of the league's goalscoring charts and attempts to replace him had mixed results. Jamie Holmes, released by Newcastle United, turned down offers from elsewhere to join the Mariners and his early-season form looked good, only for the youngster to tail away. Luke Sullivan was brought in from Consett, but ended up being loaned back into the Northern League with Bishop Auckland, while Jack Devlin barely lasted a month at Mariners Park. It was left to the experienced Graeme Armstrong, brought in mid-season from Spennymoor, and Lee Mason, signed from North Shields, to add strength in depth to the Mariners' strikeforce and both played a huge role in the run-in.

Mason hit a purple patch of form in front of goal, including a superb second half display at bottom side Goole when Shields looked on course to be on the wrong end of a major upset, while Armstrong showed all his pedigree at this level with a late winner against Skelmersdale and then a brace in the 4-0 win at Radcliffe Borough three days later which secured the title.

It had been a slog at times, but Shields had done it.

Again.

Sensationally, from those highs, fans were stunned just a couple of weeks later when Arca announced his retirement from football with immediate effect. The extra travelling and demands of life in the higher division had taken its toll on the 37-year-old, not on the pitch - his standards were still ridiculously high to the point where he was named as Evo-Stick Fans' Player of the Year and in the league's team of the season, along with Cogdon - but off it, with the Argentinian deciding to spend more time with his young family.

He had just been named the club's Player of the Year, with the exceptional Briggs taking the Players' Player award to show he had well and truly bounced back from his Wembley woe and was a player still capable of playing at a higher level.

For Picton and Fenton, promotion was another step on the right road, another justification of their methods and hard work that they've put in. Success continues to come their way, as do the admiring glances from elsewhere. Twice during the season, their names were linked with other jobs that became vacant in the region, first at Gateshead and then at Hartlepool United. Both were full-time clubs operating in the National League (the Conference, in old money) and once upon a time, they may have looked attractive propositions to ambitious managers but as things stood, South Shields was the place to be.

At the end of the 2017-18 season, Shields - operating three rungs lower - had an average home attendance that was double Gateshead's. The progress being made off the pitch continued to astound, with new facilities at Mariners Park including further stands, a huge marquee in one corner and ambitious plans for new floodlights and a potential revamp of the ground that would blow the shin-pads off anyone else at their level in the North East.

On the pitch, an FA Cup run at the start of the season had shown

Picton and Fenton that, already, they had assembled and coached a team that could compete with the big boys.

The run had all started with a 3-1 win over Bridlington Town in a game chosen by the BBC for live coverage on their red button, a further coup for the club. The cameras were treated to a stunning strike from new signing Matty Pattison, the ex-Newcastle United, Norwich City and South Africa international, who curled a wonderful left-footed effort into the top corner to help set up a clash with Witton Albion, where a Holmes double saw off the team a division higher.

It was then that the cup started to get really interesting.

A second qualifying round draw pitted the Mariners against Darlington, whose recovery from extinction had seen them reform and fly up through the leagues under Martin Gray's management to the point where they were knocking on the door of the National League. It was to be a major test of how far the Mariners had come, and one they passed with flying colours.

A week earlier, Shields' staggering 45-game unbeaten run had come to a shuddering halt in Wales at the hands of Colwyn Bay, but seven days on from that 4-2 defeat, the Mariners showed their true class with a stunning performance against Darlington.

More than 600 travelling Shields fans watched their team cruise to a 3-0 victory in the second qualifying round tie to make light of the two-division gap between the sides. If the rest of the North East wasn't too sure about how good this South Shields team really was, this was the result and performance that really made them sit up and take notice of what was happening in South Tyneside - and it was only going to get better.

Next up was a mouth-watering clash with York City, something of a fallen giant in the non-league scene. Just a couple of months earlier, they'd followed Shields onto the Wembley pitch on Non-League Finals Day and proceeded to win the FA Trophy. It was the highlight of an otherwise disastrous season that saw the Minstermen relegated from the National League and into National League North, the same division as Darlington. However, York had remained a full-time outfit and even allowing for Shields' sensational run, were firm favourites for the tie.

An incredible crowd of 2,806 piled into Mariners Park to witness one of the greatest results in the club's modern history. Just two seasons earlier, York had been in the Football League but with 35 minutes on the clock they trailed 2-0 to the upstarts thanks to Finnigan's coolly-taken penalty and a fine finish from Arca, who rolled back the years once more to show his Premier League pedigree.

Shields were in complete control, but as the game entered the second half, York's superior fitness began to tell as they pressed for a way back into the game. The full-timers capitalised on two mistakes from Shields goalkeeper Jack Norton and suddenly, in the blink of an eye, the scores were level and there appeared to be only one winner.

Shields, dead on their feet, had one last go as the clock ticked into injury time. Arca was prominent again, producing a bit of magic to earn a corner and then delivering it into a dangerous area. Robert Briggs headed it goal-wards and there was Cogdon, barely a yard out, to get the final touch and send the sell-out crowd into pandemonium.

The draw was again eagerly awaited and once more, it didn't disappoint. The biggest non-league side in the North East were now Hartlepool after their ignominious relegation from League Two a few months previous, crashing out of the Football League for the first time in their 109-year history, and having already been pitted against York and Darlington, it seemed inevitable that Pools would be Shields' next opposition.

It was to prove a challenge too far. Against a side packed with experienced ex-Football League players, Shields more than held their own for vast periods and with Pattison pulling the strings, led 1-0 at the break thanks to a Finnigan goal to give another sell-out crowd at Mariners Park hope that they could pull off an incredible feat once again.

It wasn't to be. Pools came on strong in the second half and after two quick-fire goals, including a stunning free-kick from Nicky Deverdics, they comfortably saw out the game to bring a brilliant, breathtaking cup run to an end.

It was a result that rankled with Picton and Fenton, who saw it as a golden opportunity squandered. What the cup run had done, though, was maintain the momentum from the Wembley final and the quadruple-winning season, ensured more big gates at Mariners Park and illustrated that anyone who thought South Shields may be a flash in the pan had to reconsider their views.

A high-profile FA Cup adventure, beating anything experienced by the club in that competition in a generation, and another promotion and league title undoubtedly constituted another hugely successful season and left the managers delighted with the ongoing progress.

"People said 'oh you'll walk that league'. Well, correct me if I'm wrong but Spennymoor didn't walk the league when they were in it," Picton enthused. "In their first year, they didn't get promoted. Darlington didn't walk it their first year, they didn't get promoted. At the time, they were well supported clubs financially."

Shields are now chasing those two clubs down, along with the likes of Gateshead and Blyth Spartans too. The landscape of non-league football in the region has never looked better and the new kids on the block are determined to propel themselves from the background and into the foreground of the scene.

It's a picture that is constantly evolving, however. In March 2018, Gateshead announced they were for sale, with owners Richard and Julie Bennett seeking new custodians of the club. It left the Heed facing an uncertain future. Despite a fantastic run to the FA Trophy semi-final and a high-profile manager in ex-Newcastle United defender Steve Watson, crowds at the International Stadium were dwindling and debate raged over whether the club could afford to stay as a full-time model.

Shields were even forced to put out a statement denying they were in merger talks with Gateshead. Talk about history repeating itself.

Down the A19, Hartlepool had been on the brink of extinction themselves since falling into the National League. It needed a takeover by ex-Darlington chairman Raj Singh to rescue them from potential administration and despite continuing to be a well-supported club, its financial future remains unsteady.

Singh's old club, Darlington, also went through a sticky period, losing manager Martin Gray to York midway through the season after he grew frustrated with the lack of progress made off the field. Their ownership model, where the club is under the control of the fans, may have reached a ceiling which can't be broken through without further investment being found.

It's an exciting, yet uncertain time for non-league football in the North East, one which South Shields could potentially capitalise upon. The rate of growth of a club which just three years ago was homeless, penniless and on the verge of extinction, has been breathtaking, all down to one man's vision, resources and drive.

The good news for South Shields fans is that Geoff Thompson wants to keep going.

"The first year when we won the Division Two title and the crowd went up dramatically, all of that proved that the town and the borough would get behind the club.

"It was at that point that my mind shifted a little bit to say we are on to something here, how can we develop it?

"There's a whole plethora of examples of people making these bold statements about spending money and bringing clubs on, but I do believe we are on a journey and I do think we can get back into the Football League, and certainly back into the Conference during my tenure at the club.

"We have learned as we've gone along and become more robust and more sophisticated with our planning and decision-making as time has gone on, and that has been all based on the reaction of the town and the fans because if they didn't turn up it would have all withered on the vine.

"But South Shields has got a population of just under 80,000, South Tyneside just under 160,000, so we are a big conurbation. We've already proved what we can do in a short period of time so why can't we get back into the Conference and potentially the Football League?"

The higher Shields go through the football pyramid, however, the harder the task becomes. Teams with ambition, teams with as big a fanbase - if not bigger - than their own lie in wait. There are millionaires and multi-millionaires who are trying to get their football club into the Football League. Salford City, co-owned by Ryan Giggs, Paul Scholes, Gary Neville, Nicky Butt and Phil Neville, achieved three promotions in four years to reach the National League, before dispensing with their own management duo of Bernard Morley and Anthony Johnson. You have Billericay, who hit the headlines thanks to their huge playing budget which attracted former Premier League players.

In the North East alone, Darlington and Hartlepool would love to get back into the Football League, while Gateshead have been trying to get promoted for a decade. That's before you even consider the likes of ex-league clubs Kidderminster Harriers, Stockport, Wrexham, Leyton Orient and more who stand in the way of the new kids on the block.

It's a harsh, brutal, uncompromising road that potentially lies ahead for Fenton and Picton, and they urge caution and realism from everyone connected with the club.

"It's really exciting but it has to be done everybody together, and I include the support in that," says Fenton. "If we are going to go on and achieve what the football club wants to achieve then we need the support to be as strong as ever. But we are looking forward to it, looking forward to the journey.

"You look at teams like Fleetwood and Burton, they've done it. Then the way things are going, you look at Fylde and Billericay who have got their ambitions. You have got a lot of clubs who are throwing money at it to try and get Football League status. It's well documented that it's our goal but whether we can achieve it or not is another thing.

"It's hard to put a timescale on it. The ambition this season was to get promoted and then we'll just take it from there. If you say we want to get four promotions in eight years, or whatever it may be, then it's difficult. Let's just give it our best shot."

Picton is equally as cautious. Next season, the Evo-Stik Premier League will be another tough test, even before they can consider reaching the level their local rivals are at.

"It's all one automatic promotion, one through the play-offs. It's tough. You're talking about leagues of 22 or 24 teams, that's tough. Sometimes you need a little bit of luck in your timing of going into those leagues, your promotion might coincide with another three or four clubs who are trying to do what we are trying to do with a good fanbase, a wealthy owner who can invest into the playing side. Or you might hit a year where there isn't really anyone like that in the division. Some of it is circumstantial.

"A lot of people look at Fleetwood and they went up six steps from the North West Counties League to the Evo-Stik, Conference North, Conference and now into League One. They did that, I think, in 10 or 11 years and that would be nice to achieve. There's never been a football club that has achieved six promotions in six years or even six in seven years coming from the level we're at. In my own mind, and I hope Geoff feels this way too, as long as there's that feeling that there's been progression made consistently, there will be times when we plateau for periods in terms of results and our progress on the pitch, but that's only natural as it gets tougher the higher you go.

"When you get to Conference and Conference North level you're talking about some clubs who have serious financial muscle and they are really tough leagues to get out of. You can't put a scientific model on it.

"That Conference North league is tough. York City, full-time, ex-Football League club which didn't make the play-offs. It's dead easy, it rolls off the tongue nicely - 'we want to be a Football League club again' - but there are so many other clubs out there who want to do the same.

"You just have to look at Mariners Park to see we still have a long way to go to support that, the infrastructure. Geoff has plans in place but it all takes time."

Thompson's plans don't just include the club. It's the wider community he also hopes to leave a lasting legacy for.

CHAPTER FOURTEEN

MAY 5, 2018...

Richie McLoughlin, founder, chairman, manager, groundsman and sponsor of Jarrow Roofing FC writes a letter of resignation to the Northern League.

Having invested 35 years of life - along with more of his personal money than he dares to think about - into the team, it's the end of the road. The Roof has fallen in. Not only is the club resigning from the league but it is also being folded.

The news registers a few murmurs among the South Shields FC followers. Some recall the battles on and off the pitch with an old foe, others wish him well in his retirement. There will be no statue erected at Boldon Sports Ground for a man who has dedicated his life to creating and running his own football club but he has his own legacy among the South Tyneside football scene.

Twenty-four hours later, Hebburn Town FC celebrate clinching promotion to Division One of the Northern League. It's just over 12 months since they went public over their fears for their future. Crowds were at an all-time low, money was tight and there were grave concerns over whether they could sustain a Northern League team for much longer.

Three-hundred-and-fifty-one people watched their 2-0 win over

Chester-le-Street on a glorious, scorching Bank Holiday Monday. It represented an epic turnaround in which the club had reconnected with the town, reached into the community and received so much back. New owners had come forward with big plans for the club, an ambition to create something special that would be a hub for football in Hebburn at both a junior and senior level.

Hebburn officials are happy to admit they are basing their model on what has happened a long goal-kick away at Mariners Park. The success of South Shields has given them inspiration, albeit on a smaller level, of how a club can integrate with their community, invest in the ground and develop a club that the town can get behind.

Hebburn manager Scott Oliver played for South Shields in the mid-1990s. He knows how deep a history the Mariners have but also the impact it can have on the future.

"Shields have helped raise the awareness of the Northern League and non-league football which I think has helped our crowds this season, especially if they are away. When Shields are at home, it's tough to compete with 1500 at their games but saying that we still pulled in 168 one Saturday.

"It's great to see kids and blokes wearing Shields tops. South Shields always had the feel of a big club, even when I played there in 1995. I can only see the Football League for them in the future and for me, that's good for the borough.

"Ourselves at Hebburn have set out to copy in a very small way what Shields have done, especially with social media and videoing the games. Clubs like ours can learn pretty much from everything Shields do - it is no coincidence that most, if not every club, has improved their social media side and are trying to connect more with the public."

When Mark Collingwood was appointed as Jarrow Roofing joint-manager in 2016, he spelled out the way he felt the club needed to go, saying: "We want to get this club more involved with the community. We want to be a family-friendly outfit that can engage with the local community."

It never quite happened. Roofing remained, largely, a one-man band, dependent on McLoughlin's generosity and dedication, from getting up at 5am to tend to the ground before work, to running training sessions on an evening. While he had a small band of people around him including a media department that in many ways was a trendsetter for Northern League clubs including Shields, the fanbase remained equally as small. When Richie decided to go, it was inevitable that the club would go with him.

It's an outcome that Geoff Thompson is determined won't befall South Shields when his tenure is finally over at Mariners Park. At some point, the white knight will ride off into the sunset but that will only happen once he is sure that the damsel he rescued is also safe in a castle that she owns, but has enough gold coins to pay the bills and an income stream that can keep her in the lifestyle she has become accustomed to.

Thompson has invested so much of his personal fortune, built up over decades of hard graft and jumping back up after knockdowns, that he would be more than entitled to do with South Shields Football Club as he wished. The land, the ground, the facilities, the whole structure - it is his creation.

What he plans to do, however, is sell it back to the fans.

"I see myself as a caretaker. It is great to be part of this and we are creating an infrastructure that will support Conference football. But it is all about the fans. I have a view that clubs should be fan-owned and that's not because I'm trying to abdicate, bugger off and do something else, because I would love to be involved in whatever capacity, but there are models out there.

"Dare I say it, Barcelona is a slightly extreme example but there is Motherwell, Hibs, probably a few others in the English league.

"There was no point in me getting the club back to South Shields from Peterlee and saying we wanted to get the club fan-owned when there was still nothing. So what we've done is, I've spent some of my personal money on it.

"The club has got to be profitable, it isn't yet but it's in touching distance of that.

"There's a number of our competitors who are rely entirely on the fund of the chairman. They lose sometimes approaching seven-figure sums and I've never said we will do that, and we won't. I wouldn't want to."

The football club made a loss in 2017-18, as it had done in

previous seasons, but for Thompson, that was part of the plan and he has identified 2021 as perhaps the year when he takes a step back. Before then, however, he wants to ensure the club is running smoothly from a financial and governance perspective and that everything is in place to support full-time football at Mariners Park.

Full-time football. It all seems a long way from scrapping around for enough players to make up a team at Eden Lane, letting Barrie Smith leave early so he could get to his shift at Sainsbury's on time.

In many ways, the club has already taken a big step along that route. Some of the backroom staff are full-time, with Picton and Fenton's combined roles ensuring they are hardly ever away from the club.

Taking the playing staff to that level, though, a squad of potentially 18 players and some Academy students, is a huge additional cost, but one that Thompson, managing director Keith Finnigan and marketing director David Mitchell are planning for.

The key driver will be getting fans through the gate. The crowds have shown they will come if the match is big enough and the experience good enough, but to improve the latter Thompson is determined to redevelop Mariners Park from a ground that almost 3,000 people could cram into with limited view of the pitch for some, to a mini-stadium that can comfortably house almost double that number of spectators.

A new purpose-built stadium had been explored, with a capacity of approaching 10,000, but with an estimated cost of £15million it seemed steep even for a man of Thompson's means. Instead, the plan is to redevelop the existing ground and the purchase of the vacant warehouse on the other side of Shaftesbury Avenue, estimated to have cost just under a seven-figure sum.

"There is a point where when the club is running correctly from a governance point of view, from a financial perspective, it has the right financial controls, the right infrastructure, the right fanbase, then from my point of view it then makes sense to go to the fans to see if they want to be involved.

"It will only happen when the infrastructure is finished however, and when we can support 3,000 fans at home, where people can come and comfortably watch a game. The real game-changer would be if we can build a stand opposite but there is a process we need to go through. I need to have the support of the community, the support of the council and the respect of the planning process. We have a vision though.

"Success also brings other challenges and if we get into the Conference North and ultimately the Conference there's a point during that timetable where we have to fund a full-time team. Part of the long-term thinking is about investing in the academy, and why Lee and Graham are full-time, and investing in the 3G pitch, the work we've done with the academy, plus the relationship we've now got with Mortimer College.

"Looking at season 2020-21, we want to be in a position where we can fund full-time football. When we've modelled it, we need circa 3,000 fans turning up to every home game. The key revenue drivers for the club are gate receipts, food and beverage, sponsorship, merchandising.

"When you run the numbers through this model you realise the key is getting people through the gate. We have to achieve that to run full-time football. That's how detailed our planning has become.

"We are trying to protect the football club. The land that the club purchased is about protecting the club because that land was on the market and there's not a lot we can do with the current envelope. It gives us an opportunity longer term.

"I want to create a commercial model that helps us achieve what we want without me writing cheques every month. If I had to do that all the time, as much as I love what I'm doing, it would tell me I'm getting something wrong. It wouldn't mean I was less enthusiastic about it but you have to have that right.

"When I kick the bucket the club will continue. Hopefully under my watch it's continued to develop and will be a community-owned club."

The redevelopment of Mariners Park is key to what the club is trying to achieve, something the management duo agree with.

"This place needs to go through the transformation first before we can go full-time," says Fenton. "To be able to get the fanbase up to sustain that level, we have to have better facilities in place.

"We are really, really fortunate to have the fanbase we've got but sometimes you really feel for them. If we do get 1800-2000, it's difficult to see the game. If they want to get a pint they have to queue. Logistically, we aren't where we need to be but Geoff understands that and he's got everything in place. Sometimes we wonder if we are moving too quick, but if you get a chance of promotion, you take it."

There will inevitably be some "bumps in the road", as Thompson describes them. Promotion after promotion after promotion is unlikely to keep going and it may be that there are a couple of years of consolidation needed. That is when the club will need the passionate, vocal fans to remain patient and loyal. The success of the club over the last few years has been built on many things, with the supporters a key ingredient.

"The doomsday scenario for me would be not just about hitting a bad run of results but also that the fans desert us because then it does become more of an acute problem," said Thompson. "At some point we will hit that bump in the road but we have a long-term plan.

"Shields were once a Football League side, as we all know, and I've made the point about playing Chelsea in the 1925/26 season and beating them 5-1. Those are the things that have happened in the past and it's been a number of years that the club has underperformed and not realised its full potential but if we take a long-term view, why can't the club be back in the Football League?

"This may sound like bullshit but I honestly do believe that it's possible. It may not happen in consecutive seasons, we may have a few periods where we stall for a little while. But as long as the fans are clear about what we want to achieve and they are patient then I think we'll be all right."

Doing all right on the pitch and feeling all right off it. When I first met Geoff, a couple of weeks after he had completed his deal with John Rundle, he spoke about trying to make South Shields FC a success not only off the pitch, but also in the community too. At the time, it was a vague theory of a man who had no real idea of how the club would progress, nor how quickly. Even less certain was the impact it would have on the folk of South Shields and South Tyneside, but the influence and impression the Mariners soon made on the public helped crystallize in his mind what he wanted to do elsewhere with the club.

In 2017, the club launched its very own Foundation, the charity arm of the Mariners. It was designed to get youngsters involved in sport, provide an avenue for coaches and increase the well-being of people in the borough.

In 2015, statistics revealed that 25 per cent of children in South Tyneside were overweight or obese, and two thirds of adults were in the same category, with obesity estimated to be costing taxpayers £8.6million. A year later, a report from the Health and Social Care Information Centre revealed South Tyneside had the country's second highest rate of hospital admissions as a result of obesity.

These are statistics Thompson and the board of directors have pored over. While their remit remains the progress of overseeing the first-team and developing Mariners Park, the latter now must also cater for providing a space the Foundation can call home, a true community facility aimed at helping reduce those scary numbers.

Thompson said: "As part of the ground development we are planning to build a new community development for the Foundation. That is going to be a million-pound investment in a new hub so the Foundation will have its own facility as part of the club. It will have changing facilities for the 3G pitch but it could have a dance studio, gym, cafe, something the local community can use on non-matchdays as well as matchdays.

"You look at some of the statistics around South Tyneside and South Shields around adult obesity, childhood obesity, inactivity and various deprivation indices where sadly, our town and borough rank quite low. There's no silver bullet but somebody has to stand up and try to do something, and in a small way that's what the club is trying to do.

"Sometimes in life you have these great plans and things go horribly wrong but you have to have that vision and that aspiration because if you haven't got that you don't know where you are. I didn't have this very clearly in my mind at the start but it's very clear now.

"I'm really excited about it. It's probably the most excited I've ever been professionally, it's great fun. I'm a local lad and I'd love to think that if we can create a club that is the centre of the community, and get back into the Football League, it would be an amazing thing.

"The legacy would be that we've created the club from the ashes into something that the town can be proud of."

Three years ago, the town didn't even have a football club, let alone one they could be proud of. Based 25 miles away in Peterlee, only the dedication of a hardy bunch of volunteers kept the Mariners from sinking without a trace.

Timing in football isn't just about a vital interception, a carefully-weighted pass or the run into the penalty box by an attacking midfielder. It's about having the right people at the club at the optimum moment. There are many similar non-league clubs who have suffered similar fates to what almost befell South Shields, but few of them have had the history and potential to do what this club has achieved in such a short space of time.

They've not reached the promised land just yet, but should they do so, no one should ever forget those struggles in the garden of Eden Lane.

ACKNOWLEDGMENTS

My thanks go to everyone who has helped me with the research and information that went into putting this book together.

Non-league football in the North East is a real close-knit group with a family feel to it. There have been endless people helping with the background work including Daniel Prince, Mark Carruthers and Mike Snowdon. A huge thank you also to South Shields FC club photographer Peter Talbot for the use of his excellent images that chronicle the journey the club has been on so vividly.

Thanks also go to the Ginger Owl himself, Steve Brown, for his proof-reading skills, non-league knowledge and humour, and David McCaffrey, Steve Wraith and Mick Edmondson for their patience and advice on the literary side.

Finally, connected with South Shields FC, the time given by Lee Picton, Graham Fenton, Gary Crutwell, Jon King, Jon Shaw, Barrie Smith, Julio Arca and Geoff Thompson is incredibly appreciated. But this book is for the volunteers behind the scenes, the hard-working committees not only at South Shields but at every other non-league football club where their dedication often goes without mention, praise or publicity.

They are the bedrock of football at this level and hopefully this book goes a little way to recognising their efforts.

ABOUT THE AUTHOR

Ross Gregory is a sports journalist of more than 20 years, spending just about all of his life working and living in the North East.

A keen footballer as a youngster, non-league football became his main passion after a knee injury (or eight) and he has played in the Northern League and helped coach Whickham FC where he now serves on the committee.

Professionally, he worked for the Gateshead Post and Sunday Sun before becoming sports editor at the Shields Gazette in 2007, covering non-league football in South Tyneside in his spare time.

Since 2014 he has been Head of Sport for Johnston Press North East, whose titles include the Sunderland Echo, Shields Gazette and Hartlepool Mail.

He is married with two children and two guinea pigs!

Printed in Great Britain
by Amazon